GEORGE CRABBE'S POETRY ON BORDER LAND

Gavin Edwards

Studies in British Literature
Volume 7

The Edwin Mellen Press
Lewiston/Queenston/Lampeter

Learning Resources
Centre

125 06 1 5 X

Library of Congress Cataloging-in-Publication Data

Edwards, Gavin.
  George Crabbe's poetry on border land / Gavin Edwards.
    p.   cm. -- (Studies in British literature ; v. 7)
  Includes bibliographical references.
  ISBN 0-88946-934-2
  1. Crabbe, George, 1754-1832--Criticism and interpretation.
  2. Narrative poetry, English--History and criticism. 3. Rites and
  ceremonies in literature. 4. Manners and customs in literature.
  5. Social history in literature. I. Title. II. Series.
  PR4514.E39 1990
  821'.7--dc20   89-77838
                                                                         CIP

This is volume 7 in the continuing series
Studies in British Literature
Volume 7 ISBN 0-88946-934-2
SBL Series ISBN 0-88946-927-X

A CIP catalog record for this book
is available from the British Library.

The Edwin Mellen Press   The Edwin Mellen Press
        Box 450   Box 67
  Lewiston, New York   Queenston, Ontario
      USA 14092   CANADA L0S 1L0

The Edwin Mellen Press, Ltd.
Lampeter, Dyfed, Wales
UNITED KINGDOM SA48 7DY

Printed in the United States of America

For Jean and Ted Edwards

TABLE OF CONTENTS

ACKNOWLEDGEMENTS

I am grateful to all the people with whom I have discussed Crabbe. I want particulary to thank the following, who have commented on sections or earlier drafts of the book: Kelvin Everest, Deborah Ferris, Martin Golding, Andrew Hawkey, J. Hillis Miller, Jeremy Mulford, and Christopher Ricks. Fiona Norwell and Elsie Reynolds typed early drafts of the book and Cathy Booth of Texpert Systems prepared the final copy. I am very grateful to them. I am grateful to the staff of Saint David's University College, Lampeter, for their expert assistance and to the College's Pantyfedwen Fund for a generous grant towards the preparation of the final copy. Earlier versions of portions of this study have appeared in *Essays in Criticism*. I should like to thank the editors for allowing me to use that material here.

Chapter 1

Crabbe's Poetry in History

William Hazlitt wrote in *The London Magazine* for May 1921 that 'to read him is a penance; yet we read on! Mr. Crabbe is a *fascinating* writer'.[1] The best things that have been written about Crabbe's work — and Hazlitt's essay is one of them — have expressed puzzlement. The poetry exerts a fascination which the ways of thinking we have hitherto brought to bear upon it have not been able to account for. Descriptions of his work tend to have a standard form: he is a transitional poet, a short-story writer in verse, a realist poet, 'Pope in worsted stockings', 'Malthus turned metrical romancer'. His poetry is always like something else — only quite different. The categories in which it is described are plainly not built to house him.

The one category on which the critics have repeatedly fallen back is the least illuminating in the critical lexicon, 'realist'. Anyone who has worked their way through *Crabbe: the Criti-*

---

[1] *The Complete Works of William Hazlitt*, edited by P.P. Howe, 21 vols (London, 1930–34), xix, pp.51–62 (p.53).

cal *Heritage*[2] will be aware of the extraordinary tenacity of this
family of terms: reality, fact, the literal, the actual. It is almost
as if each contribution to the volume is based on a reading of its
predecessor rather than on a reading of Crabbe.

But of course they are readings of Crabbe. Neither the
identification of Crabbe's work as a deviation from literary norms
nor its description as realistic result simply from the imposition
of alien categories on a reluctant text. After all Crabbe did offer
to show us 'the real picture of the poor', to 'paint the cot,/ As
truth will paint it, and as bards will not' (*The Village*, i.5,53–
4).[3] Crabbe says that he is a realist and implies that this makes
him — since he is a bard himself — an unusual and paradoxical
figure.

Literary critics have taken their cue from Crabbe himself.
And not only literary critics: Crabbe's reputation as a realist
has encouraged one social historian after another — from the
Hammonds to Lawrence Stone — to cite him as witness to social
conditions in rural and provincial England in the late eighteenth
and early nineteenth centuries.

If Crabbe is a realist there may not be much for literary
critics to say about him. A large part of the business of literary
critics is to analyse those formal qualities which, so it is said,
help to distinguish literature from other kinds of writing, qualities thought to be minimal in Crabbe's case. And if Crabbe
accurately records the social life of his time not much labour is
required to establish a social context for his poetry: its content
describes its context.

This book offers an historical reading of Crabbe's poems,
and it makes use of the work of social historians, among others,

---

[2] Edited by A. Pollard (London and Boston, 1972).

[3] Crabbe's poems are quoted from *The Complete Poetical Works*,
edited by N. Dalrymple-Champneys and A. Pollard, 3 vols (Oxford,
1988), subsequently referred to as *CPW*.

in order to do so. But it suggests that the poems are complex and that their relationship to their historical context is also a complex one. It takes Crabbe's own programmatic statements seriously but it does not take them as gospel. Crabbe tried to understand the society of his time and he tried to understand his own poems. But there are good reasons why neither he nor subsequent critics and historians should have been wholly successful in this respect.

Jerome McGann has recently suggested that Crabbe is 'a writer whose true historical period has yet to arrive'.[4] This may be an exaggeration. Some recent work — by Raymond Williams, John Barrell, L.J. Swingle and McGann himself — suggests that the time has now arrived.[5] We are now in a position — we have now developed some of the preoccupations and categories — which enable us to do justice to the power and complexity of his work. The readings offered in this book have to some extent been made possible by recent developments in the analysis of culture and society. Participants in these developments however are seldom readers of Crabbe, and readers of Crabbe are not usually, in my experience, interested in debates of a theoretical or methodological kind. Consequently it may be useful if I outline and exemplify, in advance, some of the principles which direct the detailed readings offered in the rest of this book.

Writing in *The Atlantic Monthly* in 1880 George Woodberry praised Crabbe's work for its

> transparency, the quality by virtue of which life is seen through the text plainly and without distortion; ... He not only saw the object as it was; he

---

[4] *The Beauty of Inflections* (Oxford, 1985), p.311.

[5] Raymond Williams, *The Country and the City* (London, 1973); John Barrell, *The Dark Side of the Landscape: the rural poor in English painting, 1730-1840* (Cambridge, 1980); L.J. Swingle, 'Late Crabbe in Relation to the Augustans and Romantics: the temporal labyrinth of his *Tales in Verse*, 1812', ELH 42 (1975), pp.580–94.

presented it as it was.[6]

Woodberry's words sound like a caricature of assumptions about
language and literature which many modern theorists have
sought to undermine. Catherine Belsey for instance sounds as if
she is answering Woodberry when she describes post-Saussurian
theory as an approach which

> starts from an analysis of language, proposing
> that language is not transparent, not merely the
> *medium* in which autonomous individuals trans-
> mit messages to each other about an independently
> constituted world of things. On the contrary, it
> is language which offers the possibility of consti-
> tuting a world of individuals and things, and dif-
> ferentiating between them. The transparency of
> language is an illusion.

In its continual attempt to repress the status of the text as a
system of signs, 'realism offers itself as transparent'.[7] The task
of the analyst is to refuse the offer; but also to demonstrate the
mechanisms by which the effect of transparency is achieved. In
a semiological perspective realism is always would-be realism.

It would seem proper that Crabbe, the realist poet *par excellence*, should have an important place in any semiological reformulation of English cultural history. The readings offered in
this book frequently resemble and in many cases are influenced
by various strands of semiology. Nevertheless I do not employ
semiological concepts in a systematic way. This may well be a
limitation, but there are in fact some good reasons for following
a conceptually eclectic course. In particular, the present work
offers to put Crabbe's poetry in an historical context, and while
Roland Barthes claimed that 'a little formalism turns one away

---

[6] *Crabbe: The Critical Heritage*, pp.451–7 (p.454).
[7] *Critical Practice* (London and New York, 1980), pp.4, 51.

from history, but a lot brings one back to it'[8] not many semiol-
ogists have yet found their way back without much crashing of
conceptual gears.

Of course I need to spell out carefully what sort of an historical context I have in mind. After all, one such context has
already been rejected: the context derived by critics and historians from the ostensible content of Crabbe's own poems. In
subsequent chapters I do indeed take what Crabbe has to say
about, for instance, poverty and sexuality in 'The Parish Register' very seriously. But I argue that what his poems say about
such matters is often hard to establish and contradictory, and
that the poems need to be seen as interested participants in,
rather than disinterested reports upon, social relationships. Indeed the poems themselves betray a continuing if often covert
and uneasy interest in their own status as representations.

Two contexts in particular should be mentioned at this
point, not because they are the only significant ones but because
they illuminate especially clearly the kind of complex relationship between text and historical context that I hope to establish
in subsequent chapters.

The first such context is suggested by the fact that many
eighteenth-century works of art exhibit two features which, in
a semiological perspective, may initially seem hard to reconcile.
They aspire towards transparency, but they simultaneously emphasize the artifice required to produce this effect. What holds
these two positions together is the view that real life itself has
the structure of a formal representation. Johnson's 'Vanity of
Human Wishes' is a case in point:

> Let Observation with extensive View,
> Survey Mankind, from *China* to *Peru*;...
> Let Hist'ry tell where rival Kings command,
> And dubious Title shakes the madded Land,

---

[8] *Mythologies* (London, 1972), p.112.

When Statutes glean the Refuse of the Sword,
How much more safe the Vassal than the Lord,
(1–2,29–32)

'Observation' is not simply the ability to see and to understand but also the ability to 'make observations', to represent. Similarly 'Survey' suggests the casting of the eyes over a scene, the assessing of it but also, simultaneously, the making of a survey, a map or written report, a representation. Consequently 'Hist'ry' conflates a kind of text (a history book) and the supposed referent of that text, the real events in the past.

What is involved here is an assumption, often quite explicit, that to see things as they really are is to see them as having the structure of a formal representation. Theatre, the visual arts, or written or spoken narrative may equally provide the terminology which embodies this assumption. For instance Crabbe, as I shall argue, commits himself to this assumption when he offers to describe not simply the reality of poverty but 'the real picture of the poor'.

Focussing on the analogy with narrative representation, Martin Golding, in an unpublished essay, has named this assumption — which he believes is pervasive in eighteenth-century moral writing — a 'narrative idea of the moral life'. Alasdair MacIntyre has talked in similar vein of a 'narrative concept of selfhood' according to which 'I am what I may justifiably be taken by others to be in the course of living out a story that runs from my birth to my death'.[9]

A standard eighteenth-century use of the word 'character' embodies these assumptions. It is a use which conflates what are for us the distinct meanings of 'personal identity' and 'figure in a narrative'. Boswell gives us Johnson's character rather than a description of his character. One's character is one's proper

---

[9] *After Virtue: a study in moral theory* (London, 1981), p.202.

description, the figure one cuts in one's life conceived as a narrative in the third person. It is one's proper description in much the same sense that a proper name is proper to the person it names; in the narrative idea of life there is taken to be far more in common between proper names and other aspects of language than we take to be the case today. And Crabbe's ambivalent attitude to this narrative idea — he was deeply committed to it and deeply sceptical of it — is manifested, as we shall repeatedly have cause to notice, in his attitude towards naming.

If Boswell gives us Johnson's character rather than a description of it, he also gives us Johnson's Life rather than a narrative of his life. A life, seen as it really is (seen 'in perspective', to adopt the vocabulary of the visual arts) has the structure of a Life. And, as we shall see, Crabbe's use of the word 'life' can be as significantly ambiguous in this respect (in 'The Parting Hour' for instance) as his use of the word 'character' (in the Preface to *The Borough* for instance).

If the use of certain common words like 'character', 'life', and 'story' seem to imply a structural identity between existence and its formal — especially its narrative — representation so too did other, less exclusively discursive features of English life. The second element of Crabbe's historical context which may usefully be mentioned at this point is that kind of deliberate formality known as 'ritual' which seems, in certain important and relevant respects, to have played a more manifestly significant role in eighteenth-century than in twentieth-century lives.

The rituals I have particularly in mind are those whose function is to mark the transition between stages of the human life-cycle. Baptism, marriage and funeral are rites of passage of this kind.[10]

Rites of passage are formal occasions, in which we play largely pre-scribed parts. They are part of what Michel Fou-

---

[10] A. van Gennep, *The Rites of Passage* (London, 1960).

cault referred to as 'the dramaturgy of the real'.[11] And as this
metaphor from theatre suggests, they have a special relationship
to dramatic narrative. For one thing, rites of passage help to
divide the continuity of existence into distinct segments and link
the segments together into a sequence. They work to convert
existence into a narrative, lives into Lives. For another thing,
a feature of such rituals which implies a specially close relationship between existence and its formal representation is the
importance within them of so-called 'performative' utterances.
Performatives, according to J.L. Austin, are utterances — like
'I name this ship the *Queen Elizabeth*', 'We find the defendant
guilty', 'I promise to support you' — which actually effect —
'perform' — the actions to which they refer.[12] They are self-
referring utterances by means of which the speaker is not simply
saying something but doing something. They are ritualistic —
formulaic — utterances, and it is in the context of ritual — in
which people act self-consciously in terms of precedent and pre-
scribed roles — that such utterances are most often and most
powerfully employed. Most of Austin's performatives come, as
the examples given above suggest, from ritual occasions of this
kind. It is by means of these ritual performatives that, for instance, a daughter becomes a wife, altering both the common
noun and the proper name by which she is known to herself and
to others. A marriage ceremony is a tissue of performatives, both
spoken and written: the signing of the register is as much an integral part of the marriage as 'I declare you man and wife'. As
Foucault said of entries in the internment registers of the Biblio-
theque Nationale, such utterances don't simply refer to reality,
'they perform in it. ... [They] played a role in this real of which

---

[11] 'The Life of Infamous Men' (1977), in *Michel Foucault: Power,
Truth, Strategy*, edited by M. Morris and P. Patton (Sydney, 1979),
pp.76–91 (p.78).
[12] *Philosophical Papers* (Oxford, 1961), pp.220–39.

they speak...'.[13]

Rites of passage, then, involve an especially strong and insistent bonding between human life and its formal representation. And to the extent that people in our own society still take part in such rites, the point holds good for English society in the twentieth as well as in the eighteenth century. But, just as we don't normally use words like 'character' and 'life' in quite the same way Boswell did, so there have been significant changes in the place of the rites of passage in our lives. They are changes which effect the strength of that bonding between life and formal representation which the rites imply.

For one thing, a smaller proportion of couples who live together have church weddings or baptize their offspring. Furthermore the legal existence and registering of a new child or a marriage or a death is now distinct from the appropriate church ceremony which thereby becomes a more exclusively religious event. What is particularly interesting for a discussion of Crabbe (who was born in 1754 and died in 1832) is the date of the legislation which effected some of these changes. It was the Marriage and Registration Acts of 1836 which made the crucial changes separating religious ritual from secular registration. The area Poor Law officer, who had taken over the parish clergyman's role in the administration of poor relief in 1832, now also took over as official registrar of births and deaths. At the same time marriage by licence could be conducted as a civil ceremony or in a non-conformist place of worship.

The state church, through the local clergy (including Crabbe of course), had controlled the rites of passage and the distribution of poor relief. However, the power of these religious-juridical rituals prior to the 1830s depended on more than administrative arrangement. Their power depended on their setting in a particular context of working and of sexual life. After all, people's

---

[13] *Michel Foucault: Power, Truth, Strategy*, p.79.

sense of their own identity and the identity of their fellows is determined quite as much by such factors as by those ritual events
whose main and explicit function is to create or modify identities.

In the course of this book I shall draw attention to various
features of everyday life which encouraged a narrative view of it
and to some features which put pressure upon such a view. But
it may be useful to mention one such feature at this point both
because it is particularly important and because it illustrates
particularly clearly the kind of historical context for Crabbe's
poetry that I wish to construct.

The historical demographer E.A. Wrigley has argued that
'in the period between Tudor and Victorian times, no significant
change occurred in the average size of the co-resident domestic
group, though significant changes did occur in its composition,
the most notable of which was probably the decline in the importance of live-in servants in husbandry'.[14] The chronology of
the decline varied regionally but it accelerated in the first two
decades of the nineteenth century and was more or less complete
in the South and East by 1830.

Servants in husbandry were wage-workers but not really pro-
letarians since — unlike day-labourers — they were normally
hired by the year and lived in their master's house under his
quasi-paternal authority. They were almost always young (young
men or young women) and one index of their status and characteristic age is that they were not supposed to marry.[15]

The institution of husbandry service had its equivalents in
urban areas and at higher social levels. Apprenticeship is the
most obvious case in point (the apprenticeship clauses of the
Elizabethan Statute of Artificers were abolished in 1814), but

---

[14] 'Reflections on the History of the Family', *Daedalus*, 106 (Spring
1977), pp.71–85 (p.78).

[15] Ann Kussmael, *Servants in Husbandry in early modern England*
(Cambridge, 1981), p.83.

the children of ladies and gentlemen were also farmed out to other households for some or all of the period between childhood and adulthood. The historian of husbandry service writes that 'families at every level of early modern society sent their children into the households of others, and families at all but the lowest levels brought others' children into their own'. Correspondingly the decline of service was a part of the polarization of classes, between the propertied and the completely property-less, between the 'servant-supplying and servant-hiring families'.[16]

What service and apprenticeship had in common was that they involved subordination of a general rather than a purely economic kind. The Master aspired to control over the whole life of the servant, not just to the purchase of his or her labour-power. Economic, familial and political relationships — which we commonly think of as distinct — were not easily distinguishable. And it is the relationship between a Master and a normally younger servant which provided the basis for the description of every kind of relationship (between, for instance, employer and day-labourer or nobleman and monarch) in the patriarchal language of Master and Servant, a language whose reality or otherwise is a fundamental preoccupation of Crabbe's poetry.

If service provided a powerful model for relationships in general it also illuminates the characteristic shape of individual lives. We tend to think that individuals are normally members, in the course of their lives, of two kinds of family. Anthropologists refer to these two families as the 'family of orientation' in which a person is brought up and the 'family of procreation' which a person forms by marriage. The system I have described suggests a social order in which there is, for most individuals, a third type of family inserted between these two and mediating between them. This mediating function is underlined by the role of the marriage ceremony itself as the formal link between service, apprentice-

---

[16] *Servants in Husbandry*, pp.9,10.

ship and its equivalents on the one hand and the formation of a
family of procreation on the other. If marriage is forbidden to
servants and apprentices it also characteristically marked their
exit from that status.

In other words the efficacy of the rites of marriage and (insofar as procreation followed marriage) of baptism depended upon
the system of farming out adolescents. Alan MacFarlane has argued that the custom 'solved the problem of what to do with
young people between puberty and adulthood'.[17] It was itself a
rite of passage. Certainly the ability of ritual performatives to
convert lives into Lives depended on their co-ordination with an
ordering of working and sexual life which itself supported the
narrative pattern.

I have focussed on religious-juridical rituals — and especially on their performative features — so as to displace two
powerful but misleading distinctions: between reality and representation, and between creative and documentary texts. All
formal representations participate in the creation of reality.

But of course they don't all participate so effectively or in
the same way. By talking about poems and weddings in the
same breath, linking them as acts of formal representation, I
don't mean to imply that they are the same. Poems, weddings,
prayers, petitions and legal judgements have distinct proper-
ties. 'The Parish Register' is not a parish register: they differ in
their readership, their form, and their function. They are both
nevertheless manifestly formal constructions whose function is
the definition and redefinition of human identities. The differences between them are very specific and — as we shall see in a
later chapter — quite as hard to define as the similarities. We
must never reduce such differences to some apparently fundamental distinction between documentary texts (which are taken

---

[17] *The family life of Ralph Jocelyn, a seventeenth century clergyman* (Cambridge, 1970), p.146.

to record a reality external to themselves) and creative texts. That distinction is itself a product of historical developments, some of which I have outlined.

So if I have criticized social historians for treating Crabbe's poems as documents this is not in order to win an academic demarcation dispute. After difficult theoretical and methodological preparation, parish registers can usefully be read as documents, for instance by historians like Wrigley and Kussmael engaged in family-reconstitution studies. But the registers were also creative works, active in the constitution of families. Correspondingly if it is wrong to treat 'The Parish Register' as a document this is because it participated in, not because it transcended, the life of its time.

My aim in this book is not to remove Crabbe from social history but to put his work in a different relation to a differently conceived history. His work participated in, and illuminates for us, certain tensions in the relationship between existence and its formal representation. And since this is a history in which acts of naming are very important (proper-naming and common-naming, taking your husband's name and becoming a 'wife') it should come as no surprise that it is partly through his use of certain everyday words that Crabbe takes part in it.

These words are of two kinds, both of which have been briefly mentioned already. Firstly, there are words like 'character' and 'life' which can refer both to features of reality and to features of formal representation. And secondly, there are words like 'servant' and 'master' which offer to describe particular positions in the social order.

Crabbe's use of the word 'servant' in 'The Parish Register' illustrates in a particularly vivid fashion some of the ways in which his poetry can be said to perform in the reality to which it refers. In the 'Marriages' section of that poem the parson argues that it is a good idea not to get married too soon: people should 'delay'. He then catalogues a number of miserable marriages,

but finally admits that there are a few happy ones. Farmers'
daughters normally become contented farmers' wives and

> not to those alone who bear command,
> Heav'n gives a Heart to hail the Marriage Band;
> Among their Servants, we the Pairs can show,
> Who much to Love and more to Prudence owe:
>   (ii.431–4)

His examples are Reuben and Rachel, who work and save for
some years before they get married, in line with the parson's
insistence that 'there's great advantage in a small delay'.

   This complex sequence will be discussed in more detail in a
later chapter. What interests me here is the word 'servant'. A
social historian might be tempted to use these lines and the story
that follows to illustrate the sexual and economic behaviour of
servants in the early nineteenth century. A radical social historian might use them to illustrate the biased views of the clergy
about the behaviour of servants. Both approaches would be misleading because both would assume — as the poem encourages
them to assume — that the word 'servant' has a clear and single
meaning. It does not.

   Ann Kussmael has traced some of the variations in the
meaning of the word. Its standard modern meaning is 'a person
employed to carry out home duties'. But in Crabbe's time 'servant', as the name for a specific social function, had two senses
neither of which coincide with our own. It could refer to 'all those
who worked for one master, and were maintained by that master'. Important among these were the 'servants in husbandry'.
A second meaning was broader: 'servant' could refer to anybody
who did manual work for somebody else, whether as a servant
in husbandry or as a day-labourer.[18]

   The word was also used — and still is occasionally used —

---

[18] *Servants in Husbandry*, pp.5–10.

in a rather more figurative sense, to describe anybody who serves a higher authority. In this extended sense a lord is the servant of his monarch, a monarch the servant of the Lord. This sense is important in some of Crabbe's poems as we shall see, but it is the two more literal senses which concern us here.

'The Parish Register' illustrates Kussmael's contention that 'the two synchronous meanings can be confusing'.[19] We cannot tell from Crabbe's description of Reuben and Rachel whether they are day-labourers or servants in husbandry. But the context in which he uses the term makes it essential that we should be able to tell. After all, servants in husbandry were almost always young people, and young people who were not *allowed* to marry. The 'delay' urged by this 'Malthus turned metrical romancer' is built into the institution of service.

By contrast, young day-labourers did not have the same incentive to delay marriage since their earning power (and therefore their ability to support offspring) would be greatest when they were young and able-bodied. Furthermore the old poor law, as it was modified by the Speenhamland decision of 1795 ensured that people did not suffer financially from the burden of extra children which early marriage would commonly involve. It might not be in the interests of parson and ratepayers that workers should marry early, but it might well be in the interest of labourers.

My purpose in introducing these historical details is to suggest some of the issues which Crabbe can evade by blurring the two senses of 'servant', and some of the reasons why he should want to do so. He can present the failure to 'delay' marriage as a widespread moral failure rather than as a rational response to altering material circumstances. And without actually denying the existence of young day-labourers he can assert the existence of a patriarchal social order in which service forms the natural

---

[19] *Servants in Husbandry*, p.6.

transition between childhood and married independence.

Neither should we think of Crabbe's usage here as a device — deliberate or unconscious — peculiar to himself. He refers in the course of 'The Parish Register' to Burn's *Justice of the Peace and Parish Officer* (1755), as a source of instruction for the parson in his capacity as Poor Law administrator. Burn says that 'the law never looks upon any person as a *servant*, who is hired for less than one whole year; otherwise they come under the denomination of labourers'. But a later chapter, dealing with all labour, is entitled 'Servants' and under this heading are discussed 'Labourers, journeymen, artificers, and servants'.

By bringing together Crabbe's lines and historical information from other sources — information Crabbe himself does not provide — we can get a special insight into certain features of historical reality. If people — parsons or magistrates or labourers or poets — think about day-labourers in the language of 'service' this must predispose them to think and act in certain ways. The ways in which people articulate their world helps to constitute that world, even if it does so by leading them to misconstrue certain important features of it.

The same examples — Crabbe's use of 'servant' in those lines — conveniently illustrates two other features of the analysis offered in this book. In the first place it should be clear that the poetry is neither a passive symptom nor a coherent analysis of historical circumstances. This is a necessary point to make at this stage because the readings that follow may sometimes seem to represent the poetry in one or other of these guises. For instance *The Village* is described in a way that suggests it is driven by contradictory forces which its author cannot fully understand, while 'The Frank Courtship' to a remarkable degree brings contradictory attitudes into open and deliberate combat. Yet the distinction between the two kinds of achievement is somewhat arbitrary. Symptoms and analyses after all are both relatively distinct from the disease itself. Crabbe's poetry, as his use of 'servant' suggests, participates in the disease. And how could it be otherwise? After all, these poems are formal representations grappling with a crisis in the relation between life and its formal representation. 'The Frank Courtship' is a remarkable achievement precisely because of the way in which it draws attention to its own and its readers' participation in this crisis.

Secondly, 'servant' was ambivalent in a rather special way. It was not simply a word with two meanings which under certain circumstances could be confused. Rather, the group of people referred to by one meaning of the word form a part of the larger group of people referred to by the other meaning of the word. As in Burn's *Justice of the Peace*, servants (in husbandry) are one kind of servant (in the wider sense). Modern feminists have argued that the word 'man' is shifty in just this way since it refers both to the human race and to a sub-group of the human race. Crabbe's poetry thrives on this rather special kind of shiftiness. *The Village* in particular, as we shall see, proceeds by categorial shifts of this kind. Indeed, the familiar notion that Crabbe's poetry combines neo-Classical generality with Romantic or realist particularity can be reformulated in this perspective: does 'the' in a title like *The Village* indicate a category or an example of that category?

It is not only through its use of complex everyday words that Crabbe's poetry participates in its historical context. Nevertheless it is always in part by scrutinizing their linguistic surface that we discover what the poems are really doing. Crabbe's remarkable narrative poems are the major case in point. Quite as much as any *nouveau roman*, they are narratives about narrative. By this I do not mean that they are not about real life; they are about the relation between real life and its narrative organization. Crabbe is committed to the assumption that to see your life as it really is is to see it as a narrative in the third person, a linked sequence of segments in which one's character exists only as the characters (or roles) one plays. But he also

suspects that there is no such solidarity between lives and Lives.
And his insecure commitment to a narrative idea of life is linked,
at every point, to his equally insecure commitment to the patriarchal language of 'service'.

Chapter 2

On Border Land

There is a girl in Crabbe's poem 'Delay has Danger' (1819) by the name of Fanny. On the death of her father Fanny goes to live with her aunt and uncle. Crabbe's confusingly meticulous description of her situation is as follows:

> She was the daughter of a priest, whose life
> Was brief and sad: he lost a darling wife,
> And Fanny then her father, who could save
> But a small portion; but his all he gave,
> With the fair orphan, to a sister's care,
> And her good spouse: they were the ruling pair —
> Steward and steward's lady — o'er a tribe,
> Each under each, whom I shall not describe.
>
> This grave old couple, childless and alone,
> Would, by their care, for Fanny's loss atone:
> She had been taught in schools of honest fame;
> And to the Hall as to a home, she came,

My lord assenting: yet, as meet and right,
Fanny was held from every hero's sight,
Who might in youthful error cast his eyes
On one so gentle as a lawful prize,
On border land, whom, as their right or prey,
A youth from either side might bear away.
Some handsome lover of th' inferior class
Might as a wife approve the lovely lass;
Or some invader from the class above,
Who, more presuming, would his passion prove
By asking less — love only for his love.

This much experienced aunt her fear express'd,
And dread of old and young, of host and guest.
                                                    (203–27)

Fanny comes to the Earl's household 'as to a home' but she is
never really at home there. She is affiliated to three families
— her father's, her uncle's, the Earl's — and a real member
of none. By the same token her class position is unclear. Her
aunt later describes herself and her husband as 'servants in a
certain way'; since Fanny is subject to them she can easily be
taken for a servant by other servants who would like to marry
her or by young gentlemen who would like to seduce her. On
the other hand she is not quite a servant: her uncle and aunt
rule over the other servants and she herself is the daughter of
a priest. She is described as 'gentle', which may mean she is a
gentlewoman.

Fanny is an anomaly in the Earl's household. And the com-
pound uncertainty about her status has as one of its main effects an uncertainty of her own about what sort of person she
is allowed to desire. This gives her an affinity with the poem's
male protagonist, the young man Henry. Henry has been sent
away from home, not completely against his will, possibly to de-
tach him from a socially unsuitable courtship. He is himself a

guest of uncertain status in the household of the Earl, who is his father's 'patron'. Fanny and Henry are fatally suited to one another.

The uncertainties which beset Fanny and Henry also have to do with the life-cycle: what stage of life has each of them reached? Is Henry, who finds he has got engaged to Fanny, already tacitly engaged to the girl back home? As for Fanny, she comes to the Earl's household 'as to a home': is this the kind of home you leave in order to get married or the kind of home you form by getting married? Fanny and Henry don't know whether they are coming or going.

Debilitating uncertainties of this complicated kind are characteristic of the situations in which young people find themselves in Crabbe's stories. The example from 'Delay has Danger' is so interesting because in it Crabbe has found a vivid metaphor for the situation: Fanny lives 'on border land'.

There are two reasons why this metaphor is particularly appropriate. One is that a similar metaphor — a metaphor of geographical transit — is used by anthropologists to describe features of human culture that are directly relevant to Crabbe's work. The so-called 'rites of passage' are, as we have seen, rituals whose function is to effect changes in status, including movements from one stage of the life-cycle to another. Such rites are composed, we are told, of three elements: a rite of separation (from an existing role, of daughter for instance), a rite of aggregation (into the role of wife for instance) and, mediating between them, a liminal stage in which one is temporarily free of any fixed status, betwixt-and-between, on the threshold itself. Crabbe's protagonists are, in effect, stuck in this liminal stage which they experience not as liberation but as debilitating uncertainty.

The second reason why Crabbe's geographical metaphor is so appropriate is that many years previously, in *The Village*, he described himself as 'cast by Fortune on a frowning coast' (i.49), an actual border where

> joyless roam a wild amphibious race,
> With sullen woe display'd on every face;
> Who, far from civil arts and social fly,
> And scowl at strangers with suspicious eye.
>
> Here too the lawless merchant of the main
> Draws from his plough th' intoxicated swain;
> Want only claim'd the labour of the day,
> But vice now steals his nightly rest away.
>
> (i.85–92)

The Greek root of 'amphibious' means 'double life', and this 'frowning coast' is the site of various connected forms of double life. The people live both by land and sea and in an unnatural way, so that while they are human beings they seem also to be animals, actual examples of the amphibians to which they are being compared. Crabbe evokes a kind of apartheid: the 'natives of the place' are a race apart. And in lines which directly foreshadow Fanny's 'border land' by linking geography and territorial conflict Crabbe describes those

> Who still remain to hear the ocean roar,
> Whose greedy waves devour the lessening shore;
> Till some fierce tide, with more imperious sway,
> Sweeps the low hut and all it holds away;
>
> (i.125–8)

As for Crabbe's most famous protagonist, Peter Grimes, he 'fish'd by water and he filch'd by land'. Cut off from human society by his cruelty and his loneliness, drawn to it by his loneliness and his greed, he is a very individual member of that 'amphibious race'. The poem takes place among salt-marshes and mud-flats, hyphenated territories which are neither land nor sea. Crabbe is always fascinated by such intermediate substances and categories. Sand and mud are sometimes part of the land and sometimes part of the sea; they are not liquid but neither are they solid ground or dry land. Grimes himself lives in a 'mud-wall'd hovel' (close kin to the 'low-built hut' of *The Village* no doubt) and most of Crabbe's characters, wherever they may actually live, seem to build their houses on sand. Was Crabbe aware, as he composed 'Peter Grimes' in his scrawly handwriting, of the curious appropriateness of his own name?

> When Tides were neap, and, in the sultry day,
> Through the tall bounding Mud-banks made their way,
> Which on each side rose swelling, and below
> The dark warm Flood ran silently and slow: ...
> Here dull and hopeless he'll lie down and trace
> How sidelong Crabs had scrawl'd their crooked race;
>   (181–4, 192–3)

Crabbe's poems are good at describing life on border land. But they are themselves often subject to the ambivalence they describe. *The Village* is an amphibious poem. The villagers are described as 'wild' and 'sullen', a 'bold, artful, surly, savage race', but also as 'the poor laborious natives of the place' (i.85,86,112,42). It is hard to reconcile Crabbe's description of them as dissolute wastrels responsible for their own poverty with his sympathy for them as the hard-working victims of natural and social circumstances. And this ambivalence is linked to another. The poem finds it difficult to co-ordinate its address to the poor and its address to the rich on behalf of the poor into a neutral position outside classes from which it can speak to both. *The Village* presents the villagers as living in a different country from the poem's cultivated readers, and the poet himself seems to stand on both sides of the border which divides those countries.

Perhaps it is not surprising that the poems should be subject to the ambivalence they describe. Borders are puzzling things. Their function is simultaneously to link and to separate. For most settled societies peaceful relations with other societies involve the maintenance of a satisfactory co-ordination of these functions. The border line itself is the focus of this difficult situation. A border line marks the distinction between two territories and links them: the line itself is a part of both territories and of neither. When you get close to it a border line becomes a border land, the potential site of a general conflict which threatens the territories — geographical, social, conceptual — to either side of it. In 'Delay has Danger' it is not just Fanny who is confused. The men belonging to a series of binary categories — the servants and the gentlemen, the young and the old, the hosts and the guests — would think they knew what she was but would be mistaken. They would be thrown into confusion because they would misread what they thought were reliable signs. Fanny threatens the signifying system within which they live, destabilizing the meanings they take for granted.

And the poem is not immune to the general confusion it evokes. 'Delay has Danger' compares interestingly with *Mansfield Park* in this respect. Austen probably named Fanny Price after a character in Crabbe's 'Parish Register' who just avoids marrying too far above her station. Whether Crabbe in his turn borrowed the Christian name back we don't know, though he certainly knew of, and had probably read, Austen's novel. In any case, the protaganists of *Mansfield Park* and 'Delay has Danger' certainly inhabit the same border land where uncertainty about one's class and family are linked to uncertainty about one's place in the life-cycle. Austen establishes the link very precisely:

> 'I begin now to understand you all, except Miss Price,' said Miss Crawford, as she was walking with the Mr Bertrams. 'Pray, is she out, or is she not? — I am puzzled — she dines at the parsonage, with the rest of you, which seemed like being *out*; and yet she says so little, that I can hardly suppose she *is*.'

Edmund and Tom both think they know the answer to Mary's question but are clearly confused by it. Uncertainty about Miss Price's class and uncertainty about the stage of life she has reached intersect to puzzle them all. The clarity with which Austen at this point represents confusion is not matched in the Crabbe poem. But this is not for lack of trying. The description of Fanny's early life with which this chapter began is meticulous in its determination to describe all the individuals involved in terms of the roles which, simultaneously or in succession, each of them plays. Thus Fanny's father is 'priest', 'father' and brother — brother to his 'sister' who is also 'steward's lady' and 'aunt' to Fanny — who is also 'daughter', 'orphan' and ward. The passage implies that you could list all the possible roles available (kinship roles, economic roles, political roles and so on) and then specify any particular person as a certain combination of these roles.

As a way of talking about people and society this is a recipe for extreme clarity. It is a kind of natural-historical tableau set before the mind's eye. And though a spacial metaphor most closely defines the sort of clarity to which it aspires, the fact of change, of temporal alteration is built into it. The sequence of a person's life would be constituted by the acquisition of new roles and the loss or subordination of old ones. For instance, when Fanny becomes a ward she remains her father's daughter; when she becomes a wife she is no longer a ward but she remains, in a subordinate fashion, a daughter.

In what way then is the passage so confusing to read? It is confusing because each person is described in terms of so many different roles in the course of a few lines. We are uncertain as we read just how many actual people are being described; it is as if 'priest' and 'father' are different people rather than different roles occupied (simultaneously) by the same person:

> She was the daughter of a priest, whose life
> Was brief and sad: he lost a darling wife,

> And Fanny then her father, who could save
> But a small portion; but his all he gave,
> With the fair orphan, to a sister's care,
> And her good spouse: they were the ruling pair —
> Steward and steward's lady — o'er a tribe,
> Each under each, whom I shall not describe.

The grammar of the sentence is ambiguous: 'her' in the third line seems to refer to the 'darling wife' so that the wife loses a father and Fanny a grandfather. There is an effect of generational slippage (as there was for Oedipus who married his mother, as there was for Freud who was born an uncle). Of course we can sort out the awkward grammar and arrive at the official story but the phantom story nevertheless unfocusses the official one. The uncertainty of Fanny's position is supposed to stand out in relief against the background of a meticulously ordered system; but the uncertainty infects every corner of the system itself so that nothing ever quite comes into focus.

One consequence of this infectious uncertainty is that we cannot be any more certain than Henry himself is as to how far he is the victim of an elaborate plot. He discovers that his casual entanglement with Fanny has been noticed, approved, and even, it would seem, planned by her adoptive parents and the Earl himself. One day they congratulate him on his engagement to her, which he did not want and did not properly believe he was leading himself into. They won't let him interrupt their enthusiastic permission on the grounds (or is it the pretence?) that it is only his youthful embarrassment which wants to deny his intimacy with Fanny. And in the course of her explanation of how the present happy event has come about, Mrs Johnson, the steward's wife, describes an audience with the Earl:

> 'We saw my Lord, and Lady Jane was there,
> And said to Johnson, "Johnson, take a chair:"
> True, we are servants in a certain way,

But in the higher places so are they;
We are obey'd in ours, and they in theirs obey —
So Johnson bow'd, for that was right and fit,
And had no scruple with the Earl to sit ...'

(598–604)

The patriarchal relationships which Mrs Johnson boasts about here are ways of establishing orderly reciprocal relationships between people via the co-ordination of the similarities and differences between them. In classic monarchical terms: the King is Father of his people but just as children and wives and servants are subject to actual fathers so the King is subject, as all children and fathers are, to Our Heavenly Father. The idea of 'service' to which Mrs Johnson refers is central to this patriarchal co-ordination of similarity and difference. For instance Thomas Broughton wrote in his *Serious and Affectionate Warning to Servants* (1746) that

It has pleased the almightly Governor of the world to make a difference in the outward condition of his subjects here below; and though *high and low, rich and poor, one with another*, are all his *Servants*, yet in the course of his providence he has thought good to appoint various orders and degrees of men here upon earth. Some of these are placed by him in a high, others in a low estate. Some are born to rule, others to obey. Hence arises the necessity that some should be Masters, others Servants: and this constitutes a mutual relation and duty between them.[1]

For Broughton, as for Mrs Johnson, it is a virtue in the word 'servant' that it can be used in these two ways, both to describe

---

[1] Quoted by R.W. Malcolmson, *Life and Labour in England, 1700–1780* (London, 1981), p.14.

some people and to describe everybody. The word's flexibility
is a source of clarity, not of confusion. The similarity between
places in the patriarchal order (we are all servants) complements
rather than contradicts the difference between those places (some
of us are servants, some are masters).

At this point it may be useful to clarify the relationship
between the double meaning of 'servant' proposed openly by
Thomas Broughton and by Mrs Johnson and the double meaning
of the same word concealed — as we have seen — in Crabbe's
usage in 'The Parish Register'. In the latter case, in 'The Parish
Register', both senses of the word constitute the title of a specific
kind of person: it is either the name given to all wage-workers
or the name given to that kind of wage-worker who works for
a whole year under the authority and supervision of one master. Here in 'Delay has Danger' we are faced with a related but
distinct dimension of this complex everyday word. We are concerned with the link between its use as the title of a specific kind
of person and its much wider and rather more figurative use to
describe a role which, in one way or another, everyone may be
thought of as playing.

The range of linked uses for which the word is available indicates its central place in a patriarchal order; that is to say, a hierarchical order in which all relationships are thought of as quasi-
familial ones. Furthermore, the fact that the most restricted and
literal of its senses refers to young people whose sojourn in the
patriarchal household is a temporary one indicates the central
position which such youthful temporary residents played in this
order in early modern England.

It is in this context that we should understand the carefully graded noble household of 'Delay has Danger'; a household
which reaches out — through ties of kin and patronage — to
incorporate Fanny and Henry. But if we do read the poem in
this context the positions of Fanny and Henry are quite *typical* of patriarchal order, not anomalous at all. And certainly

nobody in the Earl's household thinks there is anything *obviously* odd about Henry or about Fanny (that is why she causes such confusion). What makes Henry feel that his environment is uncanny and threatening is the bland insistence of everybody around him, which he partly shares, that nothing odd is happening at all. And both Crabbe and his narrator seem, to some extent, to share this perspective: hence the moralising cast of the poem's title and the concentration on Henry's moral character — his indecisiveness — as the cause of his predicament. Nevertheless the young couple's experience is powerfully infectious. The whole carefully differentiated order of the Earl's household, real and solid as it is supposed to be, is also shifty and surreal. All the relationships between different functions can seem curiously shifty: between parent and guardian and patron, between servant and master, between wife and daughter, between the steward as a master of servants and as a servant of a master who is also a servant. It is not only in Henry's paranoid ears that Mrs Jackson's complacent description of quasi-feudal reciprocities can sound theatrical and sinister. Who is the servant and who is the master? The fact that 'servant' can mean different things *does* in these circumstances — as it did in 'The Parish Register' — become a mark of confusion and not a guarantee of order.

The patriarchal order to which Crabbe wants to commit himself is one in which a person is identified by the roles which, simultaneously or in succession, that person plays: the roles, for instance, of servant, father, orphan, master. My use of the term 'roles' from the theatre is deliberate, though 'parts' would be the equivalent term for Crabbe and his contemporaries. What is involved is the assumption, sometimes quite explicit, that to see reality as it really is means seeing it as having the structure of a formal representation. I have already referred to this assumption in Martin Golding's terms, as a narrative idea of the moral life. And this should remind us that the formal representation

ged need not be theatrical: the visual arts, or written or
spoken narrative may equally well provide the terminology which
embodies this assumption.

In Crabbe's poetry it is patriarchal order which requires and
ensures the congruence between reality and representation. But
it is necessary to ask whether this link between patriarchal and
narrative order is peculiar to Crabbe or whether it is also visible
in the work of his contemporaries.

The well-known distinctiveness, even oddity of Crabbe's
writing, together with his relative personal isolation from literary, intellectual or political groupings might suggest that in
this as in other respects he is an unrepresentative figure. But I
have already offered some reasons for believing that his isolation
has been exaggerated. His historical context can be described in
a way that gives his work, at least in certain respects, a central
rather than a marginal significance. As for his specifically literary affiliations it has been frequently claimed — notably by F.R.
Leavis — that he appears a less isolated figure if we see him in
the company of his contemporary novelists rather than his contemporary poets. But the retrospective categorization of this as
the 'Romantic Period' in poetry leads us to misconstrue his isolation among poets. Crabbe is not a belated pre-Romantic but
an anti-Romantic. Crabbe and his contemporaries are clearly
wrestling with, and responding in diverse ways to, a common social and cultural situation. For instance Crabbe's preoccupation
with marginal and liminal conditions is shared by his Romantic
contemporaries. But Crabbe is less willing than they generally
are to assume that condition as his own, to see it as a source
of special insight, or to welcome its infectiousness. Crabbe is
tightly linked by opposition to contemporary poets. But the
post-Romantic exaggeration of the difference between poetry and
prose does encourage us to see a poet whose closest affiliations
in his own time are undoubtedly with prose-writers as an odder
fish than he really was.

Leavis suggested, in particular, an affiliation with Austen. I have already mentioned some preoccupations which the two writers share. And there is evidence to suggest that Austen was aware of the link. Whether or not Crabbe named the heroine of 'Delay has Danger' (published in 1819) after the heroine of *Mansfield Park* (written between 1811 and 1813, published in 1814) who in turn took her name from 'The Parish Register' (1807), Crabbe's *Tales* (published in 1812) is one of the books Fanny Price reads during her own difficult passage across border land. As the dates suggest, Austen's reference to Crabbe's book has a significance out of all proportion to its brevity. It gives a precise historical date to the action of her novel; and not just any date but a date in the period in which she is writing it. Her reference to Crabbe therefore seems to say: 'this novel is about what is happening in England now; Crabbe is my real contemporary because he is the other person who is writing about what is really happening'. Affinities with Crabbe are evident in all her novels, but especially in *Mansfield Park* where the fortunes of a patriarchal household are played out in terms of the complex interaction of real and theatrical 'parts' and come to depend upon the ability of the heroine to establish a secure 'character' for herself.

There are equally strong links (though no evident awareness of them on either side) across the ideological divide separating both Crabbe and Austen from their radical contemporary, William Godwin. Godwin's *Caleb Williams* (1794) is an especially interesting case in point. Its eponymous hero is 'received into the family' of the noble Falkland (noble, supposedly, in both senses) as his secretary. This is a patriarchal relationship in which Falkland is the orphaned Caleb's patron, employer and quasi-father. They are neither kinsmen nor lovers but their relationship has all the intimacy of a kin relationship or a sexual one and all the impersonality of an economic or a political one.

We can approach Godwin's novel in two ways. We can read it as an attack on the narrative idea of the moral life as the animating principle of a despotic and fraudulent patriarchy epitomized in the figure of Falkland. Falkland after all is overwhelmingly concerned with his 'name', with reputation rather than truth; his life is an endless process of constructing the character in which he is to appear in his Life. He models himself on fictional and historical figures so that what he says about one of these models — Alexander the Great — also applies to himself: 'He formed to himself a sublime image of excellence, and his only ambition was to realise it in his own story'. Falkland's position is written into his vocabulary: his use of the word 'story' refuses to distinguish between an existence and the narrative of an existence. If this is the ethos which Godwin and Caleb are attacking, the novel can be read as a conflict between Truth and Reputation. As such it belongs — as its explicit political affiliations would suggest — with *The Rights of Man* and *A Vindication of the Rights of Woman* in their determination to free 'men', or 'people', from the artifice — the dehumanizing but seductive costume-dramas and role-playing — of aristocratic and male-dominated society.

But it is equally possible to read the novel as an attack on Falkland and his ilk *in the name of* a narrative idea of life. After all, the aim of Caleb's actions and of the memoir in which he describes them is to communicate his true *story* (his existence as the tale of his existence), to present his true *character* (his identity as the description of his identity) at the bar of a court, or, failing that, at the bar of posterity. Caleb too is committed to Reputation. What he fears is the ease with which Reputation may part company with Truth, a separation which leaves Truth as empty as Reputation is false. And on this reading the novel is a struggle between true and false Reputation, in the great tradition of eighteenth-century attacks on vanity and untrustworthy appearance which culminates in Austen.

Caleb Williams is in fact a struggle between these two incompatible positions.[2] It is deeply complicit with the patriarchal order it sets out to expose: this is the reason why Caleb, even at the moment of his final exposure of Falkland, feels that he has been defeated by his 'noble' patron.

Crabbe is a major participant in that 'war of ideas' fought out in England during and after the French Revolution, to which Marilyn Butler has properly directed our attention. But to a far greater extent than has hitherto been appreciated this was a battle about artifice, about the relation between real life and its formal representation. Furthermore, the lines of battle were not so clearly drawn as many of the participants believed. Godwin's radicalism finds that its terms are strangely complicit with the patriarchal enemy while Crabbe, coming from approximately the other direction, arrives at a remarkably similar ambivalence. It is an ambivalence which is in evidence from the start of his writing life.

---

[2] See G. Edwards and K. Everest, 'William Godwin's *Caleb Williams*: Truth and Things as they Are', in *1789: Reading Writing Revolution*, edited by F. Barker (Colchester, 1982), pp.129–46.

Chapter 3

Picturing Reality

The Village (1783) is not a coherent poem. It is, for instance, very hard to reconcile the beginning of the poem with its ending. Crabbe starts Book One with a contrast between the grim reality of rural poverty as he has witnessed it and the rosy misrepresentations provided by pastoral poets for their wealthy readers. The wealthy, Crabbe implies, should be fulfilling their charitable obligation to the poor, not blinding themselves to the need for charity. But in the course of the poem Crabbe's position seems to shift so much that by the end of Book Two he can write in sycophantic — and quasi-pastoral — praise of Lord Robert Manners, the dead brother of his patron the Duke of Rutland. Crabbe says that Manners' example should teach the poor resignation: 'let your murmers cease,/ Think, think of him, and take your lot in peace'(ii.113–14).

Is the poem saying that the poverty of the poor is intolerable or that it is tolerable? It seems to be saying both things, with about equal determination. A full explanation of this apparent volte-face, of the true meaning and politics of this puzzling poem, would have to take more factors into account than I can deal with here. The poem itself draws our attention to the relation between what poems say and whom they are saying it to; and that is certainly one of the questions which, in a fuller discussion, would have to be addressed to *The Village* itself. After all, it is one thing to say to the rich that poverty is intolerable, quite another to say it to the poor. And it might be quite consistent — or at least an accepted form of double-standard — to tell the rich that poverty should not be tolerated and tell the poor that it should. The editors of a 'People's Edition' of Crabbe's poems published in Edinburgh in 1838 noted that although Crabbe had been termed 'the Poet of the Poor' and 'professedly preaches to the common people, the range of the circulation of his poems has hitherto been confined in a great measure to the highly educated and affluent'. The aim of their own edition was to 'introduce Crabbe to the great bulk of his countrymen'. But the question of whom Crabbe is addressing is a question about his implied as well as his actual readership. And as Raymond Williams has noted, 'the ambiguity of [Crabbe's] social and moral position — of the humane and indignant observer, who is also domestic chaplain to the Duke of Rutland — is interestingly reflected in the structure and even the grammatical case of the poem', in the shifting identity of Crabbe's 'you' and 'thou'.[1]

The easiest explanation for Crabbe's changes of position in the poem is biographical. He was living in poverty when he began the poem and in some comfort and security when he completed it. But this explanation is not completely satisfactory since both he and Burke must have felt that the poem did have a certain coherence. It is certainly neccessary to identify the tensions and contradictions which beset *The Village* but it is equally important to work out how such features could be seen as com-

---

[1] *The Country and the City*, p.92.

plementary rather than contradictory. What will be attempted
here is a detailed demonstration, focusing on parts of Book One,
of how the poem moves from one position to another, of the *way*
in which it proceeds.

As it proceeds the poem seems continually to alter the terms
of its argument. Arthur Sale, in the Introduction to his edition
of the poem, noted its 'shifts of focus, vagueness of location, and
changes of manner'.[2] Elaborating on Sale's visual metaphor —
'shifts of focus' — Donald Davie, in his poem 'Trevenen', writes

> Perhaps had Johnson lived, whose pen
> Tinkered with *The Village*, then
> Some one had upheld the claims
> Of spectacles defined by frames, ...
> But Johnson died, unwept by most,
> And left, to rule the sprawling roost,
> Crabbe's earnest, just, unfocussed page
> As prolix model to an age.[3]

Davie's puns ('spectacles' as things you look through and things
you look at, 'frames' as spectacle-frames and as picture-frames)
are, as we shall see, very intelligent ones. And if we want to
discover the logic of Crabbe's shifting position in *The Village*
the best place to begin is where Johnson's pen tinkered, at the
beginning:

> The village life, and every care that reigns
> O'er youthful peasants and declining swains;
> What labour yields, and what, that labour past,
> Age, in its hour of languor, finds at last;
> What forms the real picture of the poor,
> Demands a song — The Muse can give no more.
> Fled are those times, when, in harmonious strains,

---

[2] (London, 1950), p.xii.
[3] *Collected Poems 1950–1970* (London, 1972), p.287.

The rustic poet prais'd his native plains;
No shepherds now in smooth alternate verse,
Their country's beauty or their nymph's rehearse;
Yet still for these we frame the tender strain,
Still in our lays fond Corydons complain,
And shepherds' boys their amorous pains reveal,
The only pains, alas! they never feel.

On Mincio's banks, in Caesar's bounteous reign,
If TITYRUS found the golden age again,
Must sleepy bards the flattering dream prolong,
Mechanic echo's of the Mantuan song?
From truth and nature shall we widely stray,
Where VIRGIL, not where fancy leads the way? ...

I grant indeed that fields and flocks have charms,
For him that gazes or for him that farms;
But when amid such pleasing scenes I trace
The poor laborious natives of the place,
And see the mid-day sun, with fervid ray,
On their bare heads and dewy temples play;
While some, with feebler hands and fainter hearts,
Deplore their fortune, yet sustain their parts,
Then shall I dare these real ills to hide,
In tinsel trappings of poetic pride?

No, cast by Fortune on a frowning coast,
Which neither groves nor happy valleys boast;
Where other cares than those the Muse relates,
And other shepherds dwell with other mates;
By such examples taught, I paint the cot,
As truth will paint it, and as bards will not:
Nor you, ye poor, of letter'd scorn complain,
To you the smoothest song is smooth in vain;
O'ercome by labour and bow'd down by time,

Feel you the barren flattery of a rhyme?
Can poets sooth you, when you pine for bread,
By winding myrtles round your ruin'd shed?
Can their light tales your weighty griefs o'erpower,
Or glad with airy mirth the toilsome hour?

(i.1–20, 39–62)

Although these lines were published under Crabbe's name, some of them (lines 15 to 20) were written by Samuel Johnson and accepted by Crabbe as an improvement on his own version, which ran as follows:

In fairer scenes, where peaceful pleasures spring, .
Tityrus, the pride of Mantuan swains might sing:
But charm'd by him, or smitten with his views,
Shall modern poets court the Mantuan muse?
From Truth and Nature shall we widely stray,
Where Fancy leads, or Virgil led the way?

(*CPW*, i.p.666)

Johnson must have felt that Crabbe's views on neo-classical pastoral were sound but that his views on Virgil himself needed amending or clarifying. Crabbe's uncertainty however was sufficiently intractable to defeat Johnson's efforts at clarification. Johnson's own version is just as blurred as Crabbe's original. Crabbe seems to set Truth and Nature in opposition to Fancy and Virgil; but he could mean that Fancy and Virgil lead in opposite directions, one away from Truth and Nature and the other towards them. He could even mean that they both lead to Truth and Nature, an imaginative imitation of Virgil ('we tell the Truth about our society as he told the very different Truth about his') being contrasted to an anachronistic copying of him. Johnson's amendment seems to put Virgil firmly on the side of Truth and Nature, in contrast to the neo-Classical copiers. But Johnson too could be suggesting that we should follow Fancy rather than Virgil. In Johnson's version (as in Crabbe's) there is the fatally ambivalent phrase 'shall we widely stray': Johnson could either mean 'we shall go wrong if we follow Virgil' or 'we shan't go far wrong if we follow Virgil'.

John Barrell and John Bull offer to resolve the problem by saying that 'for Crabbe the question of whether there can ever have been a Golden Age was an academic one. What mattered was that in the eighteenth century the condition of the labourer was unendurable'.[4] Crabbe's 'Tityrus, the pride of Mantuan slaves might sing' and Crabbe/Johnson's 'If TITYRUS found the golden age again' may suggest that desire to put an inessential question to one side. But, as we have seen, both Crabbe and Johnson also try, and fail, to *answer* this question. Believing, wrongly, that he has dealt with the question, Crabbe is subsequently haunted by it. His ambivalence about Virgil and the existence of a Golden Age determines the course of his subsequent argument in ways he cannot control and of which he is not fully aware.

Crabbe wants to make a pretty sharp distinction between the True and the False. He tries to place Virgil and the idea of the Golden Age in terms of that distinction; his failure to do so means that Virgil oscillates across the supposedly clear line between True and False and that the exact nature of that distinction is never quite clear. Crabbe is on both sides of the fence: with Virgil against Virgil's imitators but against a Virgil who is classified with the imitators. Is Crabbe offering himself as Virgil's true heir, as the neo-classical writer of a mock-pastoral in which allusion to swains and groves and muses provides the perspective from which contemporary village life can be seen for the grim thing it really is? Or does he allude to these things only in order to reveal the irrelevance of all such allusion, invok-

---

[4] *The Penguin Book of English Pastoral Verse* (Harmondsworth, 1974), p.379.

ing contemporary reality as the standard by which art is found wanting?[5] He refers ironically to 'happy swains' but is he being ironic when he refers to 'declining swains'? When he writes

> What forms the real picture of the poor,
> Demands a song — The Muse can give no more.

does he mean that the Muse has inspired his song or that she has not?

Crabbe's poetry is normally discussed in terms of the co-existence within it — a happy or an uncomfortable co-existence — of neo-classical features and Romantic or realistic features. Important terms in this kind of assessment are 'the general' and 'the particular'. It is understandable that people should want to use these terms and they are helpful up to a point. But what Crabbe's poetry displays is not so much a tension between 'the general' and 'the particular' as an uncertainty about the relationship between different levels of generality. In this case Crabbe announces that his concern is 'truth' (or, in the 1823 edition of his poems, with 'Truth'):[6]

> By such examples taught, I paint the cot,
> As truth will paint it, and as bards will not:

Truth, at this point, is a painter. Elsewhere the poet himself is a singer who will represent a painting — 'the real picture of the poor' — in his song. Truth (especially with a capital 'T') is linked with pictures because it involves distancing yourself from particular circumstances so as to get them 'in perspective'. Everyday reality is confused; art allows us to distance ourselves from it so that we can see it as it *really* is. The artifice of art

---

[5] See R.B. Hatch, 'George Crabbe and the Tenth Muse', *Eighteenth Century Studies*, 7 (1974), pp.274–94.

[6] Crabbe's use of upper and lower case letters is described in *CPW*, especially i.pp.xxxi, xxxvii–viii; see also G. Edwards, 'Crabbe's So-Called Realism', *Essays in Criticism*, 39 (1989), pp.84–91.

allows us to see reality as the designed thing it really is. Hence Crabbe can present himself as a painter but also as a singer about what is already a painting.

But Crabbe's concept of 'the real picture' is nevertheless a tricky one. The picture never really comes into focus because he cannot decide exactly how his own direct knowledge of village life fits into it. There is of course no reason in principle why particular circumstances and experiences cannot exemplify truth. Indeed when he says that 'By these examples taught, I paint the cot' it is clear that the cottages he knows are seen, from the start, as members of a class, as instances of the generic cot (or 'Cot', in 1823). The problem is to decide how typical they are of the class to which they belong. Crabbe could, certainly, be saying that the cottages he knows are not only examples of 'the cot' but also, directly, examples of the 'truth', that they are typical cottages. But he could equally well mean that his knowledge of these particular cottages has taught him *that he should tell* the truth about the cot: in which case these examples of the cot are indeed an example to him in the sense that they are object lessons, but they are not necessarily typical cottages. These alternative ways of reading this couplet are of course directly related to the alternative ways of reading the passage about Virgil and the Golden Age. If Virgil was telling the truth, if the Golden Age did exist, then Crabbe's direct knowledge may certainly be a part of the truth, but a relatively limited part: the darker side of a landscape which Virgil's modern copiers conceal. But if Virgil is a liar like his copiers, Crabbe's own knowledge can offer itself far more directly as the truth, at the centre of the real picture. The lines in which Crabbe invokes life as he knows it on the 'frowning coast' are emphatic and intense. But they emphasize simultaneously two things which may point in opposite directions: the reality of his knowlege and its particularity.

So Crabbe's picture is out of focus because we cannot be sure how much of it is constituted by the scenes he is describing. How far are these scenes a close-up, a detail? How are the close-up of his own village life, the longer shot of modern English village life, and the even wider view of village life in general related to one another? To what level of generality does his own knowledge refer?

Crabbe believes that he has established, at the start of his poem, a framework which the rest of the poem will fill in. But he has in fact offered alternative frameworks, and so no clear framework at all. Consequently every detail of the subsequent argument constitutes an attempt to clarify the initial framework. As a result the picture can never be completed: the continually deconstructed framework will always open a space requiring to be filled in with more detail. This is the source of the lack of focus and the prolixity to which Donald Davie refers.

Another reason why Crabbe's concept of 'the real picture' is a tricky one is that it is not easy to distinguish as sharply as Crabbe would like us to between the real picture which truth paints and the unreal picture which bards paint. Bards are, after all, attacked for seeing village life from a distance, as an aesthetic object. They see it like tourists, like 'those who gaze'. They can see land and the people who work it as landscapes with figures because they have no first-hand knowledge of it. They can see it as a spectacle because they see it through rose-coloured spectacles stolen from Virgil. Can we distinguish the distance and the artifice which produce fantasy and false generalization from the distance and the artifice which produce true generalization? In principle such a distinction can certainly be made. Raymond Williams has argued that Crabbe presents himself, in *The Village*, as 'the humane and indignant observer'. Such an observer, whose observations (in both senses) are informed by a knowledge of what it is like to be a participant may in theory be distinguished from the observer for whom aesthetic pleasure, detached from questions of utility and morality, are ends in themselves.

Neo-classical writing implies a double movement in which one moves away from everyday experience so as to see it in per-

spective, as it really is. In what amounts to a powerful alibi
everyday experience both does and does not appear in art; the
difference between everyday experience and artistic representation can be both affirmed and denied. The exclusion of certain
features of everyday experience is justified on the grounds that
they are 'accidental' or too 'minute'. Crabbe in effect reduces
the space across which the double movement takes place so that
its status as an alibi becomes dangerously apparent.

Crabbe finds it very difficult to distinguish the positions he
is attacking from the positions he is attacking them from. His
son reports that as a child the poet used to collect contributions
to the 'Poet's Corner' from *Martin's Philosophical Magazine*,

> one of which, he used to say, particularly struck his
> childish fancy by this terrible concluding couplet:

> The boat went down in flames of fire,
> Which made the people all admire.[7]

The couplet neatly crystallizes Crabbe's own sense, in *The Village*, of the link between the aesthetic sense — the seeing of
things as spectacles or pictures — and heartlessness. Hence his
attack on pastoral poets and his sense of the natural affinity between them and their wealthy urban readers. But where does
the childish fancy of young Crabbe stand? He observes this scene
with his mind's eye and he admires the couplet. His very distance from the people and from their admiration implicates him
in their admiration — their admiration for a scene of spectacular
destruction from which they are distanced by fire and water. In
The Village too, as we shall see, the image of a crowd on shore
gazing at a ship in difficulties at sea crystallizes the problem of
perspective integral to Crabbe's enterprise.

---

[7] *The Life of George Crabbe by his Son* (1834), with an introduction by E. Blunden (London, 1947), p.13.

It has been suggested that Goldsmith's *Deserted Village* is a more radical poem than *The Village* because it offers an historical perspective on contemporary village life while Crabbe believes that what is the case here and now always was and must be the case.[8] Crabbe's realism, on this view, is an attempt to discourage utopian schemes and to persuade the poor to 'be realistic'. This is certainly one tendency in the poem and one way in which the poem could be read. But it is not true that Crabbe simply denies historical — or geographical — variation. The uncertainty in his attitude to history emerges in a particularly vivid way when he is also talking about his own life-history:

> Where are the swains, who, daily labour done,
> With rural games play'd down the setting sun;
> Who struck with matchless force the bounding ball,
> Or made the pond'rous quoit obliquely fall; ...
> Where now are these? Beneath yon cliff they stand,
> To show the freighted pinnace where to land;
> To load the ready steed with guilty haste,
> To fly in terror o'er the pathless waste, ...
>
> Here wand'ring long amid these frowning fields,
> I sought the simple life that Nature yields;
> Rapine and Wrong and Fear usurp'd her place,
> And a bold, artful, surly, savage race;
> Who, only skill'd to take the finny tribe,
> The yearly dinner, or septennial bribe,
> Wait on the shore, and as the waves run high,
> On the tost vessel bend their eager eye;
> Which to their coast directs its vent'rous way;
> Their's, or the ocean's miserable prey.
>
> As on their neighbouring beach yon swallows stand,
> And wait for favouring winds to leave the land;

---

[8] *The Dark Side of the Landscape*, pp.77–85.

> While still for flight the ready wing is spread:
> So waited I the favouring hour, and fled;
> Fled from these shores where guilt and famine reign,
> And cry'd, Ah! hapless they who still remain;
>
> (i.93–6, 101–4, 109–24)

Two times are interwoven in this passage: the long time which separates the classical world from his own and the shorter time of his own life. Each of these distinct times is confused and the confusion in each aggravates the confusion of the other.

The passage begins with a question ('Where are the swains ...?'). But we cannot tell from the answer ('Beneath yon cliff they stand...') whether the past tense of the question (of 'play'd down the setting sun...') represents a real past. The past tense may refer to what happened in classical life as well as in classical poetry, or it may refer to what happened only in classical poetry and therefore didn't really happen at all. We cannot tell whether the answer means 'this is what the swains have become' or 'this is what the so-called swains always were'. Consequently the present tense of the answer is as ambiguous as the past tense of the question: we cannot tell whether the present scene is an example of what is *now* the case (of what 'is' rather than 'was') or of what is *really* the case (of what 'is' rather than 'is not').

It is at this point that the problem is complicated by the introduction of the poet's own life-history. He tells us that, at an earlier stage in his life, he 'sought the simple life that Nature yields'. This formulation may mean that as a young man he was himself taken in by pastoral misrepresentations of village life but has subsequently realised his error; he was looking in the wrong place at the wrong time; perhaps he was wrong to look at all since 'the simple life' is a fantasy. But there is obviously an obstacle to this reading since although 'sought' is in the past tense 'yields' is in the present. The phrase 'the simple life' may sound like an ironic quotation from pastoral fantasy but it is hard to read the whole phrase — 'the simple life that Nature yields' — as ironic. Particularly since the bitterly hostile description of the local people which follows only makes sense if he really does believe that they have 'usurp'd' the 'simple life that Nature yields'; if he really does believe in the possibility or the actuality (in other times or places) of a Golden Age.

The passage argues against itself. It makes a distinction between his past deluded self and his present undeluded self but it also subverts that distinction in a way that suggests he may not have been deluded then or that he may still be deluded now. Ostensibly he is a native of the place who subsequently left it and now returns as an observer. But since he contrasts himself with 'the natives', refers to himself as 'Cast [there] by Fortune', and still seems to be searching there for 'the simple life' the official chronology is threatened by another according to which he never really inhabited the village and has never really left it. He is, like the swallows, a permanent migrant. As for the local people they are condemned for failing to live up to an image which they themselves reveal to be no more than a pastoral fantasy. It is not surprising then that the very strong feelings displayed in the poem are so insecurely attached to their objects, that the same local people described here as a 'surly, savage race' are described elsewhere as 'the poor, laborious natives of the place'. Can they really be the same people?

Even within this passage there is some doubt as to how far and in what sense the village people described in the first and second paragraphs are the same people. Obviously the people he saw as a young man are unlikely all to be exactly the same individuals he sees now on his return. Crabbe's point would seem to be that they are culturally and morally the same people, people of the same *kind*. The curious grammar of the long sentence which constitutes the second verse paragraph emphasizes this essential identity: the savage race who 'usurp'd' the simple life become, later in the sentence, the people who 'wait' on the shore.

This continuity suggests that, however specific this present scene may be it is also a typical scene, an instance of what happens as well as of what is happening. The temporal reference of this present-continuous tense — of 'what happens' — would seem to be the span of the poet's own life. This present (the present of the poet's life-span) can of course be linked to the present of 'Beneath yon cliff they stand' in the previous paragraph. But we have already noticed that *that* present can be understood as referring to a universal reality — 'this is what village life is really like wherever and whenever you look'. Consequently, although it is possible to read 'Wait on the shore' as an example of what is now happening this reference to the immediately contemporary present may also be read as a reference to 'what happens' in the most universal sense.

But of course, as we have seen, 'Beneath yon cliff they stand' may refer to what happens nowadays *rather than* what happened in Virgil's time; and if Nature really does, in general, yield the simple life then the present tense of 'Wait on the shore' refers very much to what is true at this moment and may even be significantly different from what was the case in the poet's youth. Can we say with confidence that the crowd described in the first paragraph are engaged either in the same activity as, or in a different activity from, the crowd described in the second paragraph? The crowd who stand beneath the cliff 'To show the freighted pinnace where to land' are presumably smugglers. The crowd who 'Wait on the shore, and .../ On the tost vessel bend their eager eye' could be smugglers too, described in rather different terms; but they could equally well be waiting for an innocent trading vessel to be wrecked, perhaps a vessel they themselves have lured onto the rocks. Smuggling and wrecking were both known on the Suffolk coast through the eighteenth century and both were illegal (though keeping flotsam from a wreck was not). But if we want to know whether these are, morally speaking, the same people, whether they are the same 'kind' of people, we need to know more about what the second group are actually doing.

Crabbe wants to present the truth, the 'real picture'. He wants to produce a poem governed by a universalizing present tense to which distinctions between past and present — between 'what was the case' and 'what is now the case' — would be subordinate. But a number of factors, including the flexibility of the present tense (which may refer to what is really the case or to what is now the case) allows for ambivalence in this project. And Crabbe needs this ambivalence because — as the passage we have been examining suggests — he is not sure which of two normative truths he wishes to commit himself to: that the village life is typically dreadful or that Nature typically gives the simple life. The awfulness of his own village is in principle compatible with either truth — but in the first case as a typical example, in the second case as an untypical example. In order that he need not make up his mind between these two incompatible truths he exploits the inherent flexibility of the English present tense.

He also exploits the inherent indefiniteness of the so-called definite article. And to some extent the character of the place he is talking about at the beginning of the poem co-operates with the latent ambivalence both of the present tense and of the definite article:

> Ah! hapless they who still remain;
> Who still remain to hear the ocean roar,
> Whose greedy waves devour the lessening shore;
> Till some fierce tide, with more imperious sway,
> Sweeps the low hut and all it holds away;
> When the sad tenant weeps from door to door,
> And begs a poor protection from the poor.
>
> (i.124–30)

Does the definite article in 'the low hut' and 'the sad tenant'
— or, for that matter, in the poem's title — name an individual
or a category? Presumably the latter. And insofar as the image of an individual is suggested it is an individual example or
image or embodiment of a category. But the circumstances described are so curious, must involve so few huts and such a small
number of people that we may indeed suspect that Crabbe is
actually talking about a single hut which is still, after all these
years, threatened by the sea rather than about a type of hut
which is so threatened. If this were so, the sweeping away of
the hut would be a single, a unique event rather than something
which 'happens'. This uncertain convergence of the singular and
the plural, of what is happening and what happens evokes the
experience of trauma and obsession, of a singular event which
happens over and over again.

Crabbe has difficulty in co-ordinating a sense of the continuity of his own life, or of the village life, with his sense
of the alterations that may have affected them. And what
is true of time and history is also true of space and geography. But he is more explicit about geographical variation.
Having described life on the 'frowning coast' the poem continues:

> But these are scenes where Nature's niggard hand
> Gave a spare portion to the famish'd land;
> Her's is the fault if here mankind complain
> Of fruitless toil and labour spent in vain;
> But yet in other scenes more fair in view,
> Where Plenty smiles — alas! She smiles for few,
> And those who taste not, yet behold her store,
> Are as the slaves that dig the golden ore,
> The wealth around them makes them doubly poor:
> Or will you deem them amply paid in health,
> Labour's fair child, that languishes with Wealth?

Go, then! and see them rising with the sun,
Through a long course of daily toil to run;

(i.131–41)

To which the first edition of 1783 added:

Like him to make the plenteous harvest grow,
And yet not share the plenty they bestow.

(*CPW*, i.p.161)

By introducing these 'other scenes' Crabbe seems to have found
a way of reconciling the belief that the life he knows on the
'frowning coast' is typical of village life and that it may be quite
untypical of it. He divides the unitary category 'the village' into
two sub-categories, the coastal village and the inland village. By
analogy with the categorial system of natural history, the village
is the genus, of which the inland village and the coastal village
are species.

But of course the generic village is itself one of a pair, contrasted with the village as it is falsely represented (and with the
town). The inland village has to be distinct from the coastal
village but also to share qualities with it — as a species of the
same genus — which can distinguish it from the village as it is
falsely represented. So Crabbe says that the inland village is
'more fair', but only 'in view' and only for a 'few'. If you work
as a labourer it's as bad if not worse than the coastal village.
Crabbe blames 'the few', or the economic system which works
to their advantage for the misery of the inland labourers in contrast to the misery of the coastal labourers which he now blames
on 'Nature's niggard hand'.

Crabbe's strategy here produces as many problems as it
solves since what he says in this passage about the causes of
poverty is difficult to square with what he has previously said on
the subject. He now says that 'Nature's niggard hand' caused
poverty in the coastal village whereas previously he blamed 'Rap-

ine and Wrong and Fear ... / And a bold, artful, surly, savage
race' who 'usurp'd' the 'simple life that Nature yields'. Only by
reading that last phrase as totally ironic can we reconcile the two
judgements of Nature and of the causes of coastal poverty. Secondly, it is hard to tell to what extent, in blaming 'the few' and
the economic system for inland poverty Crabbe is distinguishing
inland from coastal life. There must have been landowners or
considerable farmers on the coast to provide 'the annual dinner'
but their presence is not emphasized. Were they absentees from
the village as well as from *The Village*? There were certainly
farmers on the 'frowning coast':

> I grant indeed that fields and flocks have charms,
> For him that gazes or for him that farms;
> But when amid such pleasing scenes I trace
> The poor laborious natives of the place,

But this is a curious identification. By linking 'him that gazes'
with 'him that farms' Crabbe suggests that employers are in a
position to see the village life as a spectacle — as 'scenes' — in a
way that links them with tourists, townsfolk, and pastoral poets.
In a similar way 'the few' in the inland village are able to see village life as a 'view'. Up to a point this is a very radical analysis,
linking the various groups who are not direct producers together
as 'consumers' of the land, literally and figuratively, materially
and aesthetically. But the association of coastal farmers with
townsfolk and poets is taken so far that its radical thrust is undermined. The farmers are actually contrasted with 'the natives
of the place' as if they are indeed outsiders. One consequence is
to play down the issue of class conflict in the countryside in the
interests of that more conventional distinction between town and
country which is the staple of Book Two. And when 'The Village'
reappeared over twenty years later as part of *Poems*, Crabbe was
clearly concerned to further discourage a socially radical reading
of his early work, cutting out the couplet on wage-slavery, 'Like

him to make the plenteous harvest grow,/ And yet not share the
plenty they bestow' (*CPW*, i.161–2).

By contrasting the coastal farmers with 'the natives of the
place' Crabbe ensures that we cannot tell what kind of distinction if any is being suggested between the social composition and
structure of the two species of village. As with the group(s) of
people gathered on the shore to smuggle/wreck we cannot tell
where difference ends and similarity begins. What is generic and
what is species-specific?

The same problem affects the remainder of Book One in
which Crabbe describes the inadequacy and cynicism of those
parish officers and institutions which are supposed to have a special care for the poor. The descriptions clearly aspire to some
kind of representative status but, after the movement from the
coastal to the inland village, it is not clear exactly how or of
what they are representative. It seems most likely that they are
representative of the generic village. But possibly they are more
directly related to the inland village than the coastal village.
After all these descriptions of poorhouse, doctor and parson immediately succeed the description of the inland village; and if
the coastal village is the kind of place which has no resident
gentry it could also be the kind of place that has no real parish
administration.

These may seem pedantic considerations. But they are considerations which seem to have worried Crabbe or at any rate
some of his readers. In a footnote to the 1807 and subsequent
editions of the poem he wrote, apropos of the parson who fails
to turn up at the pauper's funeral:

> Some apology is due for the insertion of a circum-
> stance by no means common: that it has been sub-
> ject for complaint in any place, is a sufficient rea-
> son for its being reckoned among the evils which
> may happen to the poor, and which must happen

> to them exclusively; nevertheless, it is just to re-
> mark, that such neglect is very rare in any part
> of the kingdom, and in many parts is totally un-
> known.   (*CPW*, i.p.167)

This curious statement only underlines the poem's uncertainty.
Partly a reaffirmation, partly a bow to accuracy, partly apos-
tasy (*The Anti-Jacobin Review* congratulated him on it), it emphasizes how close the connection is between uncertainties in
Crabbe's political posture, uncertainties about geographical variation, and uncertainties of language and categorization.

In this case Crabbe feels that he has implied that parsons
never turn up at the funerals of paupers, that the scene in his
poem can be read as typical in this very literal sense. Consequently he feels he has exaggerated or mis-stated the grimness of
village life. But the corollary of this exaggeration is an exagger-
atedly rosy view in other respects. The poor people who are subject to the parson and the doctor are all very innocent victims.
Indeed, despite Crabbe's reputation for being 'Nature's sternest
painter' he has described as particularly miserable conditions in
the village poorhouse which differ very little from the conditions
of most East Anglian cottagers in his time. Furthermore Crabbe
has excluded from his poorhouse two groups who would certainly
have been there: prostitutes and able-bodied labourers. In the
light of facts of this kind, W. K. Thomas has concluded that
'Crabbe never shows much concern for proportion'.[9] But in fact
it is questions of proportion — of how different degrees of detail,
different focuses and perceptions can be made to constitute the
'real picture' — which harrass the poem. The question of 'proportion' is simultaneously a formal and a political question. At
this point in the poem Crabbe has moved from group pictures of
the village poor, or inland village poor, to portraits of particular

---

[9] 'Crabbe's View of the Poor', *Revue de l'Université d'Ottowa*, 36
(1966), pp.231–8 (p.232).

types. But this shift of attention is in fact to type-figures representing a specific sub-category of poor people. They are not close-ups of 'those who dig the golden ore' but of those who cannot do so: the pauper, the old, the sick, all traditional objects of charity and easy objects of sympathy. This double shift of attention — from groups to portraits, from labourers to the disabled — conceals the actual process of pauperization, the process by which the able-bodied poor (not just the old, the sick, the temporarily unemployed) could become permanently dependent on the parish. But this concealment of the presence of the able-bodied in the poorhouse could well have been, in Crabbe's view, a bow to another kind of accuracy. He could have believed that what he must have known in this respect was not 'typical' — of 'the village life', of coastal village life, of inland village life or whatever category of village life he believes he is presenting to us.

Chapter 4

Crabbe's So-Called Realism

A central feature of post-Saussurian literary theory has been the refusal to accept realism — whether as a literary project or a critical concept — on its own terms. Realism can only ever be 'realism', an effect of realism, so-called realism.

One of the things which is now repeatedly said is that the claims of realism are always circular. That is, a text successfully appears to represent a prior reality only because that reality is already, covertly, conceived as a text. The pre-textual realities always turn out, when you get to them, to be textual. It's a game of hunt-the-referent which you always lose. Some people enjoy losing; some people find the circles vicious.

What certainly looks like critical circularity is to be found in Frank Whitehead's Introduction to his selection of Crabbe's poetry. Commenting on 'Advice, or The Squire and the Priest' from the 1812 *Tales*, Whitehead suggests that the 'Squire in the poem

combines in his own person all the traits most
commonly to be found in members of his particular social class.   In fact, this tale 'Advice',
taken as a whole, epitomizes in a quite remarkable way a whole chapter of English social history.   All the salient aspects are there, and each
is given its due weight — the manners, morals
and outlook of the eighteenth-century squire, the
relationship between the Church and the aristocracy, the impact of the Evangelical movement, even the eventual outcome of the conflict.

Whitehead's argument is surely circular.   He can assert that
Crabbe's narrative accurately represents a historical reality only
because he has already attributed to this reality the characteristics of a narrative text: past reality is a book, divided into 'chapters' and populated with genre figures such
as 'the eighteenth-century squire'.   Whitehead then continues:

It is, no doubt, a perception of this quality in
Crabbe that has led the social historians to take
more interest in his work than most literary critics
have done.[1]

At this point we are referred to a footnote which reads:

See, for instance, the Hammonds' tribute in *The
Village Labourer*: '... Crabbe, to whose sincere
and realist pen we owe much of our knowledge of
the social life of the time'.

---

[1] *George Crabbe: Selections from his Poetry* (London, 1955),
pp.23–4.

The reference to J.L. and Barbara Hammond's *Village Labourer* is presumably supposed to provide external corroboration for Whitehead's assessment of Crabbe but in fact it does the opposite. Insofar as the two historians 'owe much of their knowledge' to Crabbe in the first place, Whitehead's argument for Crabbe's accuracy is undermined rather than, as he believes, underlined. Whitehead's own circularity is now extended so that he and the Hammonds in effect collude together to mount a further circular argument, again fuelled by the concept of realism. Whitehead depends on the historians' judgement; the historians depend on a prior literary-critical or formal judgement — Crabbe's 'sincere and realist pen'.

However, it doesn't do to be too superior, since it is easy to find oneself moving in the same circles, as I did in my reading of another 1812 poem, 'The Frank Courtship'. This tale is about a family named Kindred, leading members of a small Congregationalist or Independent sect, described as

> a remnant of that crew,
> Who, as their foes maintain, their Sovereign slew;
> An independent race, precise, correct,
> Who ever married in the kindred sect;
> No son or daughter of their order wed
> A friend to *England's* King who lost his head;
> *Cromwell* was still their Saint, and when they met,
> They mourn'd that Saints were not our Rulers yet. ...

> Neat was their house; each table, chair, and stool,
> Stood in its place, or moving mov'd by rule;
> No lively print or picture grac'd the room;
> A plain brown paper lent its decent gloom;
> But here the eye, in glancing round, survey'd
> A small Recess that seem'd for china made;

Such pleasing pictures seem'd this pencil'd ware,
That few would search for nobler objects there —
Yet, turn'd by chosen friends, and there appear'd
His stern, strong features, whom they all rever'd;
For there in lofty air was seen to stand,
The bold Protector of the conquer'd land;
Drawn in that look with which he wept and swore,
Turn'd out the Members and made fast the door,
Ridding the House of every knave and drone,
Forc'd, though it griev'd his soul, to rule alone.
The stern still smile each Friend approving gave,
Then turn'd the view, and all again were grave.

                                              (33–40, 47–64)

This did not sound to me like something which Crabbe
had invented so I spent some time looking in history books
for evidence of curious practices and devices of this kind
among late eighteenth-century dissenting communities. I could
find very little evidence that Cromwell was a significant an-
cestor for them, let alone anything as specific as what I
was looking for until I read Christopher Hill's biography
of Cromwell, *God's Englishman: Oliver Cromwell and English History.* Hill says that there is not much evidence
available about Cromwell's posthumous reputation but that
'the poet George Crabbe in 1812 described in moving lines
"a remnant of that crew ..."' and so on, concluding that
'it is hard to believe that Crabbe was inventing'.[2] Searching for a referent for Crabbe's text I only succeeded in dis-
covering Crabbe's text again. My hunch that Crabbe is
describing something that really existed was put in question by the first piece of evidence that seemed to support
it.

---

[2] (London, 1970), pp.271–2.

But if circularity inevitably accompanies realism, that circularity can take a variety of forms. The claims which Frank Whitehead is making for 'Advice' are rather different from the claims which I and Christopher Hill are making about 'The Frank Courtship'. Hill and I believe that Crabbe has a specific family, or house, or concealed picture of Cromwell in mind, or at least that he is combining elements from one or two such people or things. We suspect that Crabbe is writing non-fiction in all but name — writing, that is, about people and things as real and specific as Cromwell himself and leaving out only the name of the place and family. Whitehead on the other hand does not seem to be suggesting that 'Advice' is non-fictional; indeed if it is to 'epitomize' a chapter of social history it will probably need to be fictional in a thoroughgoing way.

One objection to the concept of realism is simply that it is rather vague, too inclusive, and does not encourage us to make important distinctions between, say, fiction and non-fiction. Indeed this over-inclusiveness often infects the semiological critique of realism as well. Common sense would insist, with some justification, that my search for a specific referent for those lines from 'The Frank Courtship' was naïve not on philosophical grounds but on empirical ones. The problem was not that I had confused signifieds and referents but that I had not looked for referents hard enough or in the right places. I should have looked not in modern history books but in old diaries, dissenting records, old houses, museums, antique shops. The only systematic attempt I know to discover specific referents for Crabbe's poems are those conducted by W.K. Thomas in his essays on the earlier poems, *The Village*, 'The Parish Register' and *The Borough*. In 'Crabbe's *Borough*: The process of Montage' Thomas sets out to investigate the common assumption that Crabbe's borough is based on his home town, Aldborough. He soon discovers that the poetic borough is much larger than Aldborough was. It has far too many inns, with the wrong names. It has substantial ship-

building operations which Aldborough, in Crabbe's time, didn't.
The tombs and bells in the poetic borough's church don't correspond to those in the church at Aldborough, and so on. None of
this may seem surprising: Crabbe is, we tell ourselves, constructing and 'epitomising' what he believes to be a typical sea-port
borough to contrast with a typical inland borough. He is aiming
at the kind of realism attributed to him by Frank Whitehead.
But the case is not so clear as that. Thomas also discovered
that Crabbe did not invent those features of the poetic borough
which cannot be traced to Aldborough. Having searched through
East Anglia, the towns and villages of East Suffolk in particular,
Thomas reports as follows:

> ...it would appear conclusive that when Crabbe
> came to enlarge on Aldborough, he did so, not
> from invention, but from his varied experience. All
> kinds of bits and pieces of observations he had
> made in scattered places he brought together, and
> from them constructed the Borough ... we can
> trace the site and natural scenery of the borough
> to Aldborough; the size of the borough, the general
> number and appearance of its streets, and its ship-
> building docks to Woodbridge; most of its inns to
> Ipswich; its various schools to Aldborough, Wood-
> bridge, Framlingham, and possibly any of Bottes-
> ford, Saxmundham, and Beccles; and its church
> to several places. In fact the borough's church
> is a mosaic in miniature, with the number and
> 'solemn sound' of its bells coming from Beccles,
> Grantham, Bury St. Edmunds, and Leicester; and
> inside the church, the tombs and effigies from the
> church at Bottesford. Undoubtedly, if the evidence
> were available, we would find that many other as-
> pects of the borough are likewise composites drawn

from several different sources, and that the borough as a whole is, even more than we can now realise, a vast montage, the product of an active compounding imagination working with the memory of observed facts.[3]

This evidence of Crabbe's commitment to specific real-life raw materials does tally with my own experience of reading the verse, even though I know nothing about these raw materials. The description of the church, like the description of the Kindred's room in 'The Frank Courtship', does not produce a clear overall picture. Instead detail is added to contiguous detail in what is often a self-defeating attempt to construct an exhaustive picture. It is as if the details have been removed from various original contexts but haven't quite made themselves at home together in their new context.

But what are these details made of? To ask the question is to realize that common sense has once again lost at hunt-the-referent. Are these details, lifted from Crabbe's experience, *real* church bells and effigies on tombs or are they *descriptions* of church bells and effigies on tombs? Thomas's analysis must mean either that the poem is made of bells and effigies rather than language or that the Beccles bells and the Bottesford effigies are made of language rather than of metal and stone. Thomas says that the poem is constructed out of 'bits and pieces of observations Crabbe has made' — an evasive formulation in which the word 'observations' is conveniently ambiguous. It can mean sights, perceptions, things seen, but also statements and propositions. It is ambiguous in much the same way that Frank Whitehead's use of the word 'history' was ambiguous, and Thomas's argument has turned out to be similarly circular. The phrase 'bits and pieces of observations he has made' is crucial to his argument, but so are the two metaphors from other arts which

---

[3] *University of Toronto Quarterly*, 36 (1967), pp.181–92.

Thomas uses: *mosaic* (the borough's church is 'a mosaic in miniature') and — a metaphor from film-making — *montage*. Each metaphor, in its own way, obscures the relationship it appears to illuminate: the relationship between the poem and its supposed referents. The bits and pieces of glass and stone which are physically transferred from various previous contexts to form the elements of a mosaic can only be accurately compared to the bits of *language* which go to make up the poem: the relationship between the language and its supposed referents remains unresolved. As for the film-making analogy, the raw materials reassembled in montage are reels of still-photographs. Roland Barthes argued that in photography humanity encountered for the first time in its history messages without a code. If this is true, then photographs are direct traces of the physical realities which they also, in various respects, resemble. Since it is precisely these direct traces and elements of resemblance — these indexical and iconic signs — which are not normally present in language, the feeling, with Crabbe's language, that in some way they almost are present is something which remains to be explained.

The feature of Thomas's analysis which points to an answer is his use of proper names. The paragraph quoted is full of them: Woodbridge, Framlingham, Bottesford, Aldborough, and so on. One characteristic of proper names is that they are tied to specific referents more tightly, more compulsorily, than most other elements of language. For instance, there are numerous different ways of talking about George Crabbe, but they all involve mentioning George Crabbe. George Crabbe is not just what I or you call him, it's what he is called. Furthermore, it's not what any other poet is called; it's not really a category. And it's what he is called in French as well as in English: proper names resist translation more successfully than any other element of language. It is therefore understandable and indeed inevitable that Thomas's argument should be full of proper names. How else could he identify the specific referents of Crabbe's descriptions except through their use? And one implication of his doing so is that he is simply reversing Crabbe's own procedure. In order to construct the descriptions of the borough's church Crabbe obviously had to remove the identifying names from his descriptions, if he was to avoid turning his church into a sale-room or a museum.

The phenomenon of the proper name may help us to redefine Crabbe's so-called realism. His language breaches the border we now normally presume to exist between the characteristics of the proper name and of other elements of language such as the common noun. It is *like* the proper name while paradoxically making us feel its *absence*. What kind of language can it be in which the proper name seems to be everywhere and yet is nowhere to be found?

Various other uses of language could be mentioned in this connection. A riddle, for instance, equals or is an elliptical substitute for that name which is absent and which it is the purpose of our reading or listening to discover. A parable is an indirect answer to a direct question ('Who is my neighbour?'). A phenomenon close to the riddle and the parable equally pertinent to the present case is mentioned by Roman Jakobson in his influential essay 'Two Aspects of Language and Two Types of Linguistic Disturbance'. He cites an aphasic patient suffering from 'similarity disorder' (associated by Jakobson with the metonymic pole of language and with literary realism) who, when presented with the picture of a compass could only respond 'Yes, it's a ... I know what it belongs to, but I cannot recall the technical expression ... Yes ... direction ... to show direction ... a magnet points to the north'.[4] I shall now try to show that the special kind of 'realism' Crabbe's poetry seems to exhibit does have to

---

[4] Roman Jakobson and Morris Halle, *Fundamentals of Language*, revised edition (The Hague, 1971), pp.69–96 (p.80).

do with its special relationship to the proper name.

The 1812 tale 'The Confidant' tells the story of a woman (Anna) who is desperate to conceal from her husband (Stafford) a guilty secret from her past (the secret is that she gave birth to an illegitimate child many years before; the child subsequently died). Anna is being blackmailed by a 'friend' (named Eliza) from that secret past who has discovered Anna's whereabouts and makes herself at home with the previously happy couple. Determined to discover the cause of his wife's increasing discomfiture Stafford conceals himself behind a curtain in

> that Room
> The Guest with care adorn'd, and named her Home:
> To please the eye, there curious prints were plac'd,
> And some light volumes to amuse the taste;
> Letters and music, on a table laid,
> The favourite studies of the Fair betray'd;
> Beneath the window was the toilet spread,
> And the fire gleam'd upon a crimson bed.
>   (420–7)

This passage is part of a lengthy narrative which, like all the tales in the 1812 volume, has no named or foregrounded narrator at all. I have felt able to summarize part of the tale precisely because the narrative seems to be 'objective'. The authority of the narrative does not of course imply that the guest's room could only be described in the actual words and phrases which are in fact used here to describe it. If we read the tale as non-fiction we must believe that the room could be described in somewhat different terms as well as in these terms. If we read it as fiction — as if the mind's eye is the only eye that could ever see this room, as if these actual words conjure the room into the only existence it can ever have — it is nevertheless quite possible that at another point in the narrative the same room could be described from a rather different point of view and remain, clearly, the same room. In both cases of course there would almost certainly be some overlap in the descriptions — words like 'and' and 'room' would probably have to recur — but the overlap could well be quite limited. In short, the willing belief that this room exists depends on the assumption that it is distinct from this particular representation of it.

Later that same evening, having discovered the truth, Stafford tells the two women a story about a Caliph, an Eastern Tale whose plot closely resembles Anna's secret life, the blackmail and his own discovery of the facts. Then Stafford says:

'My tale is ended; but, to be applied,
I must describe the place where Caliphs hide:'

Here both the Females look'd alarm'd, distress'd,
With hurried passions hard to be express'd.

'It was a closet by a chamber plac'd,
Where slept a Lady of no vulgar taste;
Her Friend attended in that chosen Room
That she had honour'd and proclaim'd her Home;
To please the eye were chosen pictures plac'd,
And some light volumes to amuse the taste;
Letters and music on a table laid,
For much the Lady wrote, and often play'd;
Beneath the window was a toilet spread,
And a fire gleam'd upon a crimson bed.'

(566–79)

This passage is likely to surprise us as much as the two women. They are surprised by the similarity between the friend's room and Stafford's ironic description of the room where Caliphs hide. We are surprised by the uncanny similarity between the husband's description of the room and the poet's description of the room earlier in the poem, and in particular by the final couplet of each passage.

What Stafford says is uncanny because of the reciprocal effect which his description of the guest's room and the containing narrative's earlier description of the room have on each other. The very close resemblance between the phrasing of the two descriptions is surely supposed to guarantee the objectivity and authority of Stafford's description by aligning it with the authority of the containing narrative. But the actual effect is to suggest either that Stafford has overheard the containing narrative (just as he overheard the two women talking), or that Stafford is a ventriloquist who actually spoke the narrative in which his own narrative is supposed to be contained. In any case, the impersonal containing narrative comes to seem, retrospectively, like somebody talking, a narrator who has a speaking part in his own narrative. Stafford's lengthy narrative is supposed to be contained within the narrative which is the poem, as a subordinate element of it. The effect of the repetition is to suggest an impossible turning inside out of this subordination, or rather to undermine any relationship of subordination in this respect.

But why should it be odd for Stafford to repeat the narrative's description so closely? It is odd because it radically alters the relationship we had earlier presumed to exist between the description and what it describes. A relationship which we had assumed was relatively optional (so that the room could have been described in quite other phrases without becoming a different room) now seems to be substantially compulsory. The earlier description is no longer simply a description of how the room can be described or was described; it is the room's proper description, its name, what it *called* (in the sense that a town is called Aldborough if that is its name). But although the first description of the room is retrospectively impregnated with the status of a proper name, the fact that neither description really is a proper name makes the effect seem odd, uncanny. It is as if the room has no real identity without these phrases being attached to it, just as a town does not have a full existence as a town without its name. A repetition which is supposed to prove the absolute independent reality of the room in fact suggests that the room may only exist as the words which ostensibly describe it.

If the room had originally been described as 'the guest-room' and Stafford had used some phrase like 'Caliphs hide in guest-rooms', the two women would still have got the message, but the effect would not have been uncanny for the reader — or at least any momentary surprise we might feel at the repetition would have been easily explained away. A guest-room would be the accepted designation for a certain type of room and we could believe that everybody in that household might refer to that room as 'the guest-room'. 'Guest-room' may not be a proper name in itself but in the context of its use between members of a household where there is only one example of such a room the phrase would function as one. It is evident then that the idea of truth which the poem espouses and which proper names embody equates truth with consensus: the true identity of a person is what they 'are called', the truth about a room is how it 'is described'. But it is not possible to believe that

> Beneath the window was a toilet spread,
> And a fire gleam'd upon a crimson bed.

is a compulsory designation of this kind. To do so would involve believing that the three people in the poem regularly used this sentence in conversation, or that the room was furnished with phrases rather than with furniture or that the poem is made of furniture rather than with phrases.

If this reading of these passages from 'The Confidant' is correct it would seem that Crabbe is not in full control of what his poetry is doing: its logic escapes him. But it does not completely do so. He is certainly interested in the relation between proper names and other aspects of life and language since this

interest is explicit in those very passages from 'The Confidant'.
The containing narrative describes

That Room
The Guest with care adorn'd, and named her Home:

making it clear that for Eliza naming her room her 'Home' was
an integral part of her campaign to dictate terms to the rest of
the household. She wants Anna and Stafford to think and speak
of the room as 'Eliza's Home', and thus turn her description
into the room's proper name. The fact that the human battle
waged in the household has been partly a linguistic battle of
this kind, a battle which Eliza has now lost, is indicated by the
word 'proclaim'd' which Stafford substitutes for 'named' in his
description:

that chosen Room
That she had honour'd and proclaim'd her Home;

Only heads of households can make such proclamations effective, Stafford implies. Crabbe shows a keen interest here in the
politics of naming, its performative character, naming as the successful or attempted establishment of a consensus. If the poem's
logic escapes Crabbe it is simply because his own language —
apparently authoritative because apparently disinterested — is
revealed as having a particular interest, the interest of the head
of the household, at heart.

   Another of the 1812 poems, 'The Lover's Journey', is also
preoccupied with the proper way to name things. John (alias
Orlando) sets off one day to visit his 'Laura' ('Call'd Susan in
the parish-register'):

First o'er a barren heath beside the coast
Orlando rode, and joy began to boast.

'This neat low gorse,' said he, 'with golden bloom,
Delights each sense, is beauty, is perfume;

> And this gay ling, with all its purple flowers,
> A man at leisure might admire for hours;
> This green-fring'd cup-moss has a scarlet tip,
> That yields to nothing but my *Laura*'s lip;
> And then how fine this herbage! men may say
> A heath is barren, nothing is so gay;
> Barren or bare to call such charming scene,
> Argues a mind possess'd by care and spleen.'
>
> (34–45)

Orlando, like Stafford, seems to quote from the narrative which contains his own speech; he quotes, in order to question, the containing narrative's term 'barren'. The effect is not quite the same as in 'The Confidant' however, not so odd. This is because the phrase 'a barren heath' is a truly commonplace phrase. It is the normal expression of the common-sense view of an infertile heath. And these are the terms in which Orlando criticizes the description: it is only what 'men may say'. But is what 'men may say' also, for Crabbe, the truth? Is 'barren', being what any such heath is called, therefore its proper name? It would seem so, on the evidence of these lines. Orlando's view is clearly the view of the tourist, the lover and the pastoral poet, 'those who gaze' as Crabbe put it in *The Village*, who see land as a series of landscapes rather than as a source of material subsistence. On the other hand the poem begins:

> It is the Soul that sees; the outward eyes
> Present the object, but the Mind descries;
> And thence delight, disgust, or cool indiff'rence rise:
> When minds are joyful, then we look around,
> And what is seen is all on fairy ground;
> Again they sicken, and on every view
> Cast their own dull and melancholy hue;
> Or, if absorb'd by their peculiar cares,
> The vacant eye on viewless matter glares;

Our feelings still upon our views attend,
And their own natures to the objects lend;
Sorrow and joy are in their influence sure,
Long as the passion reigns th' effects endure;
But Love in minds his various changes makes,
And clothes each object with the change he takes;
His light and shade on every view he throws,
And on each object, what he feels, bestows.

(1–17)

The story that follows seems to offer a clear step-by-step exemplification of this philosophical/moral formulation. Orlando rides to meet his Laura and responds to his environment in the way we have seen. He then arrives at her house only to be told that she has gone to see 'a friend'. He then rides to the friend's house through rich meadowland which he sees as 'a vile prospect'. Finally Orlando discovers that the friend is only a lady friend: the exhilarated couple retrace Orlando's steps blind to everything but each other.

We know that Orlando is deluded because the poem offers us its own objective descriptions of the scenes through which he passes to compare with the descriptions which pass through Orlando's mind. But the poem's initial formulation suggests that Orlando's way of seeing is not deviant: everybody, we are told, projects their feelings on to what they see. The initial formulation is a statement of a universal truth about perception. So where do the poem's objective descriptions come from? As we have seen, these objective descriptions are the voice of common sense, they are what 'men may say'. But this does not solve the problem since the initial formulation tells us that common sense is likely to be as deluded as Orlando's deviance. So perhaps Orlando is right to say:

Barren or bare to call such charming scene,
Argues a mind possess'd by care or spleen.

In fact the only grounds on which the superior status of the normal description can be upheld is that it is not a way of 'seeing' at all in the literal sense. What Orlando doesn't understand is that the word 'barren' describes infertility as well as ugliness. Common sense — the collection of commonplaces of which 'the barren heath' is a part — refuses to distinguish between utilitarian judgements and aesthetic ones. People who live and work in the place may indeed see the heath as ugly because their minds are 'possess'd by care and spleen'; but their minds are 'possess'd by care and spleen' because their feelings really do derive from their relationship with the infertile heath; Orlando's joy (or his 'care and spleen' when he passes through the rich meadowland) derives not — as he thinks — from his relationship with the heath but from his relationship with Laura.

So Crabbe does believe in common sense — the equation of the normal way of describing things with the true way of describing things, the narrowing of what we now take to be the distance between proper names and other features of language. And he does believe that Orlando is deviant, that the unusual way of describing things is the wrong way of describing them.

Nevertheless common sense, the notion that there is a single true way of describing things which is the normal way of describing things, is put in question by the poem; though not so much by individual delusion and deviance as by social class. Orlando is sickened by the rich meadowland: "... there's nothing seen/ In this vile country but eternal green; ..." (260–1). He despises the pride of the overfed farmers; and as for the labourers, "Theirs is but mirth assum'd, and they conceal,/ In their affected joys, the ills they feel; ..." (258–9). Orlando's feelings are delightfully understandable. They are also supposed to be wilful and perverse. But the supposedly disinterested description of this inland countryside, which precedes the description of Orlando's response to it, surely threatens to undermine the clear distinction between truth and fantasy which it takes for granted:

> Forth rode *Orlando* by a river's side,
> Inland and winding, smooth and full and wide,
> That roll'd majestic on, in one soft-flowing tide;
> The bottom gravel, flow'ry were the banks,
> Tall willows, waving in their broken ranks;
> The road, now near, now distant, winding led
> By lovely meadows which the waters fed;
> He pass'd the way-side inn, the village spire,
> Nor stopp'd to gaze, to question, or admire;
> On either side the rural mansions stood,
> With hedge-row trees and hills high-crown'd with wood,
> And many a devious stream that reach'd the nobler flood.
>   (232–43)

To describe the heath as 'barren' was to offer a simultaneously economic and aesthetic judgement of it. Just the same is true here. But it's hard not to notice that this economic judgement is now clearly a class one. The metaphors — 'majestic', 'high-crown'd', 'nobler' — are royal and aristocratic; they help to construct a scene that resembles the landscape paintings that would hang in those rural mansions. But of course they are not really Crabbe's metaphors. They are dead metaphors, commonplace ways of talking about visual beauty which the whole poem — and particularly Orlando's subsequent outburst — can bring to disturbing life. The epithets used to describe the land imply (as 'barren' implied) that criteria of aesthetic beauty and of economic utility are inseparable. But although Crabbe is committed to this conflation his poem nevertheless leads us to ask: useful to whom?

Stafford's narrative is Stafford speaking and Orlando's narrative is Orlando speaking. But the narratives which contain these two speeches are not spoken by anyone. Nobody is speaking because these containing narratives represent 'what is said'. They are spoken by anybody and by nobody. They have the same status as a 'character', the proper description of what they describe. The description of Anna's room or the description of the heath as 'barren' can be repeated by anyone because they are tied tightly to what they describe in the way we associate with proper names. They have that incontestable authority. Indeed, the convergence of the containing and the contained narratives in 'The Confidant' is supposed to be the guarantee of Stafford's authority, and the divergence between the containing and the contained narratives in 'The Lover's Journey' is supposed to demonstrate Orlando's lack of authority. But this ostensibly clear hierarchical relationship between containing and contained narratives is, as we have seen, covertly questioned. We are allowed to overhear, in the supposedly impersonal and disinterested authority of the containing narratives, the partisan voices of husbands, caliphs, kings, and nobles.

Chapter 5

The Parson Poet

The voice which John Clare thought he heard speaking in Crabbe's poetry was the voice of the parson, as he explained to John Taylor in 1821:

> I have seen 1 Vol of Crabb (last winter) called 'Tales' I lik'd here & there a touch but there is a d—d many affectations among them which seems to be the favorite play of the parson poet ... whats he know of the distresses of the poor musing over a snug coal fire in his parsonage box — if I had an enemey I could wish to torture I woud not wish him hung nor yet at the devil my worst wish should be a weeks confinment in some vicarage to hear an old parson & his wife lecture on the wants & wickedness of the poor...[1]

---

[1] *The Letters of John Clare*, edited by M. Storey (Oxford, 1985), pp.137–8.

John Clare was a labouring man so his judgement has real authority. But he is not the only person to identify Crabbe as the 'parson poet'. When people do that they don't just mean that he was a parson as well as a poet, they mean that his poetry is parsonical. Of course some of them have more positive qualities in mind than the ignorant sermonizing that strikes John Clare. But the connection between Crabbe's two callings has been notably invoked by radical critics who, like Clare, identify a definite class interest in Crabbe's supposedly disinterested realism.

William Hazlitt wrote in *The Spirit of The Age* (1825) that Crabbe's

> song is one sad reality, ... Literal fidelity serves
> him in the place of invention; ... His poetry has an
> official and professional air. He is called in to cases
> of difficult births, of fractured limbs, or breaches
> of the peace; and makes out a parochial list of ac-
> cidents and offences. He takes the most trite, the
> most gross and obvious and revolting part of na-
> ture, for the subject of his elaborate descriptions;
> but it is Nature still, and Nature is a great and
> mighty Goddess! It is well for the Reverend Au-
> thor that it is so. Individuality is, in his theory, the
> only definition of poetry. Whatever *is*, he hitches
> into rhyme.[2]

John Barrell points out that this last phrase 'indicates, by its absolute use of the verb "to be", the correspondingly absolute, unconditional 'reality' of Crabbe's world, and emphasizes the point by echoing Pope's dictum ... that "whatever is, is right".'[3] Hazlitt believes — rightly according to Barrell — that Crabbe's is the pipe-puffing realism of parochial authority urging us to

---

[2] *The Complete Works of William Hazlitt*, xi, pp.159–69 (p.164).
[3] *The Dark Side of the Landscape*, p.85.

forsake utopian schemes and 'be realistic'. The poetry, with its 'professional air' is really the voice of the impersonal parish officials, the professional classes, the doctors, parsons, magistrates, the literal and metaphorical 'overseers' of the poor. Raymond Williams talks about *The Village* in a similar vein. The stance of the 'humane and indignant observer' is finally indistinguishable from the stance of parson and doctor, 'Crabbe's own men', of those who 'care for soul and body, within the consequences of a social system'.[4]

This radical critique of Crabbe's ostensibly disinterested realism is illuminating. There are undoubtedly affinities between Crabbe's poetry and the social position of parsons, doctors and so on. Clare and Hazlitt and Williams suggest some of these affinities. But there are problems about all analogies of this kind. Firstly we need to be clear that in most such cases a *double* analogy is involved. Three things rather than two things are being linked: the verse with its air of disinterested authority, the parson's (or doctor's, or magistrate's) activities and view of life, and Crabbe's own employment as a parson (and doctor and magistrate). If we know that the author of 'The Parish Register' as well as its narrator was a Reverend we are, in a sense, likely to *miss* the force of Hazlitt referring to him as 'the Reverend Author'. What is remarkable is the convergence of the three factors. After all, there were plenty of parsons who wrote poetry quite unlike Crabbe's. If we don't keep this in mind we are likely to fall into a by now familiar kind of circularity. Hazlitt's essay, wonderfully illuminating as it is, involves circular argument. He addresses himself in effect to two distinct questions which are covertly allowed to act as each other's answer. The first question is 'Why is Crabbe a realist?' to which the answer is 'because he is a parson (or doctor, or magistrate)'. The second question is 'Why does Crabbe write from the vantage point of

---

[4] *The Country and the City*, pp.116, 118, 115.

the professional positions which he actually occupies?' to which the answer is 'because he is a realist'.

The real connections between Crabbe's work as a parson and as a poet are more complex. Certainly, the New Testament parable — that indirect and fertile method of sermonizing — was a principal source for Crabbe's work as a parson and as storyteller. In addition, the parson occupied a central position in the everyday construction of existence as a narrative. A parson, like a doctor, is a participant observer in the life of society. Parson and doctor (Crabbe of course was both) are Johnson's 'Observation' made flesh. The parson was affiliated to the propertied classes but also claimed to stand somewhat apart from all classes, linking society and its members to God. His special access to the intimate lives of his parishioners depends upon this distance from them (the analogy with the doctor is again evident). His sacred and his secular roles and powers overlap. In both respects he is an impresario of procedures through which the identities of himself and his parishioners are continually constructed and reconstructed: notably the procedures of charitable and statutory giving and the rites of passage. His position as participant-observer is a model for everybody else. A full-time participant-observer (a parson, perhaps more than anybody else except a doctor, is always his role) he is the major means by which everybody else is enabled or forced to be a participant-observer in/of their own lives. It is through the eyes of the officiating parson that people see themselves, whether they like it or not, as others see them.

Undoubtedly Crabbe recognized some of these links between his practice as a parson and the kind of poetry which he was writing before he ever became a parson. Indeed if we think we are unmasking Crabbe simply by identifying his poetic stance with his social position we should think again. Crabbe has got there first. It is not clear that Hazlitt appreciates the point since we cannot tell whether he is referring to Crabbe's work in general or specifically to 'The Parish Register' with its reverend *narrator*. Crabbe must have believed he could resolve problems encountered in *The Village* by adopting a persona that embodied participant-observation, but which was not really a persona at all because it was the persona he had already adopted in his non-writing life. Introducing *The Borough* three years later Crabbe warns that the reader

> will find the author retired from view, and an imag-
> inary personage brought forward to describe his
> Borough for him: ... the inhabitant of a village
> in the centre of the kingdom, could not appear in
> the character of a residing burgess in a large sea-
> port;... (*CPW*, i.344)

If we adopt Crabbe's terminology we can say that he appears in 'The Parish Register' 'in his own character'.

Real Crabbe may be distinct from fictional narrator but this is not supposed to undermine their essential resemblance: real Crabbe is, like the parson-narrator's imagined successors, 'one like me'. As if to emphasize the resemblance the name on the title-page of *Poems* (1807) in which 'The Parish Register' first appeared is not George Crabbe but The Revd. Geo. Crabbe, LLB. Finally, it might be expected that we could at least dis-tinguish between the real parson-*poet* and the fictional parson-*narrator*. But the fictional parson-narrator is also a poet:

> The Year revolves, and I again explore
> The simple Annals of my Parish-poor:
> What Infant-members in my flock appear,
> What Pairs I blest in the departed year;
> And who, of Old or Young, of Nymphs or Swains,
> Are lost to Life, its Pleasures and its Pains.
> No Muse I ask, before my views to bring
> The humble actions of the Swains I sing. —

How pass'd the Youthful, how the Old their days,
Who sank in sloth and who aspir'd to praise;
Their Tempers, Manners, Morals, Customs, Arts,
What parts they had, and how they employ'd their parts;
By what elated, sooth'd, seduc'd, deprest,
Full well I know — these Records give the rest.
$$\text{(i.1–14)}$$

Crabbe seems to believe that his own work as a parson provides
him with a solution to some of the problems of *The Village*. He
can dispense with the Muse unambiguously this time, because
reality already presents itself to him, in his Parish Register, or-
ganised into 'records' and 'annals'. Life is a book organized into
sections named Beginning, Middle, and End.

It could be argued that a Parish Register is itself only a representation; a representation furthermore which tells us about
village life as the parson sees it and not as his parishioners may
see it. But the Register is not just a representation of a prior
reality. Writing in the Register is an integral part (a legally required part) of the rituals whose successful completion the book
registers. The Register, as we have seen, is a 'performative' document: the writings in it, like the language of the ritual as a
whole, perform the actions (of baptism, of marriage) to which
they refer. These words are imbued with power. It is a power
which is certainly exercised over people by Church and State
through the parson who is agent of both. But it is an exercise of
power which can only be effective if people accede to it, are en-
rolled as agents in the narrative organization of their own lives.
On these occasions they must come to see themselves as public
figures, as the parson sees them. Even before photography was
invented weddings were waiting to be photographed.

It is of course the language of the marriage service as a
whole and not just the writing in the Register which is performative. The rite effects the changes of status to which it refers.

But if this is so Crabbe's decision to base the organization of his poem on the organization of the Register will have an *ambiguous* effect on his commitment to a narrative idea of life. Life may appear to the poet already organized into 'annals', but the poem reveals the mechanisms — both the parochial and poetic mechanisms — through which lives are constructed as Lives. Crabbe may write 'in his own character' but at the price of revealing tensions between different senses in which the term 'character' may be used. The poem reveals the forces which *resist* the social process of characterization. It reveals tensions between all those elements which go into the construction of the parson himself as an embodiment of Observation: tensions between the participant and the observer, between secular and spiritual functions, between the affiliation to the propertied class and the distance from all classes. 'The Parish Register' displaced rather than resolved the problems encountered in *The Village*.

Parson and poet are perhaps most interestingly linked through their relation to proper names. Both are involved in the application of names to people who, without these names would have an incomplete or blurred identity. The performative character of proper names comes out most clearly in the rite of Christening and in the acquisition of a new surname by a woman when she marries.

In 'The Lover's Journey' the pastoralizing 'Orlando' calls his lover 'Laura' but

> Fancy and Love that name assign'd to her,
> Call'd *Susan* in the parish-register;
>
> (22–3)

'In the parish-register' is supposed to be a circumlocution for 'really'. But the confident distinction between the real name and the lover's poetic name is insecure precisely because who you really are *is* what you 'are called'. Truth rests, the poem implies, on a consensus; a consensus which may be insecure even if, like a Parish Register it embodies parental, legal and theological authority. 'Call'd Susan in the parish register' means just what it says and no more.

It may even mean less. Even if 'The Lover's Journey' is read as a largely non-fictional poem Crabbe must have already altered some things. He wrote to Mary Leadbeater in 1816:

> Yes! I will tell you readily about my Creatures, whom I endeavoured to paint as nearly as I could & *dare* for in some Cases I dared not. This you will readily admit: besides, Charity bade me be cautious: Thus far you are correct. There is not one of whom I had not in my Mind the Original, but I was obliged in most Cases to take them from their real Situations & in one or two Instances, even to change the Sex and in many the Circumstances.[5]

Crabbe seems to alter his 'originals' very little and a great deal, just as the alteration of Susan to Laura is a small and a very significant alteration. The relation between people's identities and the language in which they are represented is clearly a very complex matter and Crabbe is half aware of that fact, absorbed by it.

If the two lovers in 'The Lover's Journey' have constructed their own consensus according to which Susan is really Laura, the poet has constructed a consensus with his readers according to which a girl whose name we don't know is called Susan. If this girl really existed she was *not* called Susan in a real parish register — she might even have been called Laura!

However, my problem in writing about 'The Parish Register' (and the next three chapters are principally concerned with that poem) is not so much with the names of the parishioners as with

---

[5] *Selected Letters and Journals of George Crabbe*, edited by T.C. Faulkner with R.L. Blair (Oxford, 1985), p.203.

the name of the parson, or rather 'the parson'; no amount of so-
phisticated theory about real authors, implied authors, narrators
and so on can provide us with an unambigious nomenclature. By
writing 'in his own character' Crabbe has produced a garment
which is not seamless but which cannot be neatly unstitched either. In the detailed discussions of 'The Parish Register' which
follow, 'the parson' will mean rather different things in different
contexts. Sometimes I shall try to register these differences by
referring to 'the early nineteenth-century parson', or 'a parson',
or 'the parson-poet', or 'the narrator' or 'Crabbe'. But just as
we are not dealing with an identity sufficiently homogeneous to
be properly named as 'the parson' nor is it sufficiently heteroge-
neous to be separated into a number of discrete identities.

The problems of identity — of naming and categorizing —
emerge with particular force in the poem's pronouns. The uncomfortable relationship between the person who writes, the people who are written about and the people who are written to is
evident (as it was in *The Village*) in the personal pronouns. In
'The Parish Register' the crucial words are 'we' and 'our'. In the
following passage the parson sums up his introductory picture of
village life and prepares to tell us about particular entries in his
Register:

> Such are our Peasants, those to whom we yield
> Praise with relief, the Fathers of the Field;
> And these who take from our reluctant hands,
> What *Burn* advises or the Bench commands.
> Our Farmers round, well pleas'd with constant gain,
> Like other farmers, flourish and complain. —
> These are our Groups; our Portraits next appear,
> And close our Exhibition for the Year.
>
> (i.269–76)

The first thing to notice here is a gradual shift in the referent of
the possessive pronoun 'our'. In the first four lines 'us' is perhaps

the vestry or more generally the rulers of the village, people who pay poor rates. So 'our' is defined by contrast with the various categories of village poor and with 'you' the readers. The next 'our' — 'Our Farmers round' — can't be quite the same since it refers in the third person to a group — the farmers — who must have been part of 'us' in the previous lines. This doesn't sharply distinguish the farmers from 'us' but it does mean that 'us' must refer to the whole parish — not just the ruling groups but also the various types of poor who were excluded by the previous usage.

In the final couplet 'these are our Groups' seems to mean something like 'these, which I have just been describing, are the social groups in this village'. But that paraphrase is retrospectively disturbed by

> our Portraits next appear,
> And close our Exhibition for the Year.

The complement of 'groups' in the sense of social groupings might be 'individuals'. 'Portraits' — and 'Exhibition ' — make us read 'Groups' in its pictorial sense, as 'group portraits'. This slight, almost invisible dislocation suggests a difficulty in the relation between reality and its artistic representation which we have noticed elsewhere in Crabbe's work. But what is particularly interesting in the present context is the effect of this dislocation on the possessive pronoun. 'Our' can still refer to the parish as a whole. But it can also refer to a grouping which includes the *reader* along with the poet and perhaps the parish. The pictures in the exhibition pass before everybody's eyes — reader's, parson's, poet's, parishioners' — at the same distance even if some of these people are represented in the pictures and some are not.

There are various elements in this situation: different social groups within the parish, the parson himself, and his national (but socially limited) readership. There are overlaps and divergences between these elements. At one point two of them may be linked to exclude the others; at another all may be linked, the parson-poet may link himself at various points with some as against others. None of this is disturbing in itself. And Crabbe thinks he can write as if any of the possible permutations are consistent with the narrative idea of life in which each of us can stand back so as to see life, including our own life, in perspective.

What disturbs this project is not so much the shifting *referent* of 'our' but its shifting *meaning*. Emile Benveniste has argued that the single signifier 'we' can really relate to one of two signifieds (Benveniste is discussing French pronouns but in this instance his formulation applies equally well to English).[6] This so-called 'first-person plural' is not a collection of 'I's' but a combination either of 'I plus he (or she, or it, or they)' or of 'I plus you'. The different signifieds don't just indicate that different people are linked to the speaking subject but that there is in the two cases a different orientation towards the act of speech itself. In the first case ('I plus they') 'we' links 'I' and 'they' in an address *to* 'you'. In the second case ('I plus you') 'we' links 'I' and 'you' in a way that either implies an excluded 'they' or (if the human race is being addressed) no real 'they' at all. In the first case 'you' is external to 'we', in the second case a part of it. Under cover of the unchanging signifier, Crabbe moves from an address to the reader in which 'our' means 'I the parson plus they the ratepayers' to an address which tries to incorporate 'you the readers, they the parishioners and I the parson' into a unified 'our'.

Since one of the elements which shifts under cover of the unchanging signifier is the unmentioned 'I' we might explain Crabbe's discomfort by saying that the parson-poet has got

---

[6] *Problems in General Linguistics*, translated by M. Meek (Coral Gables, Florida, 1971), pp.195–204.

caught on his hyphen. After all, one obvious distinction between parson and poet is their audience. A parson may attempt
to speak — in his sermons for instance — to all classes but he
only speaks locally, in his parish; the poet writes to a national
audience, but only to the reading classes.

Lines such as these certainly register the strains in the relationship of parson to poet. At the same time we must remember
not to confuse this relationship with others which seem to resemble it: between real and fictional author, between Crabbe and
his narrator. All these people, after all, are parson-poets.

Chapter 6

Groups

'The Parish Register' is divided into three Parts: 'Baptisms', 'Marriages', and 'Burials'. The present chapter deals with the two hundred and seventy-six lines which introduce both 'Baptisms' and the poem as a whole. It is worth noting the peculiar position which these lines thereby occupy. A part of 'Baptisms', they nevertheless have no more to do with baptisms than with marriages. They are about poverty and they attempt to divide the village poor into two groups, the deserving and the undeserving. The economic prudence urged on the poor in these introductory lines is of course easily linked to the sexual prudence urged on them in the remainder of 'Baptisms'. But sexual prudence preoccupies 'Marriages' too. The introductory lines are therefore awkwardly placed, an introduction to the tripartite 'Parish Register' and a component of one of those three parts. In a category-confusion characteristic of Crabbe, these two hundred and seventy-six lines are on the edge of 'Baptisms', inside it and outside it, occupying two positions in the poem at once.

The deserving poor are called 'th' abstemious few', 'th' industrious Swain' and 'the Fathers of the Field' while the undeserving are referred to as 'the thoughtless herd', embodiments of
'Vice and Misery'. One thing which these designations have in
common is the assumption that social categories and moral categories are the same thing. This conflation presumes that people
tend to get what they deserve: people's material circumstances
and social status are a consequence of their moral character.
Thus

> Toil, care, and patience bless th' abstemious few,
> Fear, shame, and want the thoughtless herd pursue.
>
> (i.29–30)

But the parson is not only a social analyst and moral commentator. He is also a participant in the society he describes
and categorizes: he baptizes, marries, and buries people. He
acts upon his social and moral judgements and attempts to *enforce* the co-incidence between morality and status which he describes. And this is as true of his work as chairman of the Vestry
— reponsible for the administration of parochial charities and
Poor Law relief — as it is of his more strictly religious functions:

> Such are our Peasants, those to whom we yield
> Praise with relief, the Fathers of the Field;
> And these who take from our reluctant hands,
> What *Burn* advises or the Bench commands.
>
> (i.269–72)

But there is some tension, as we shall repeatedly have
cause to notice, between his functions as social analyst,
moral commentator, priest and parish administrator. For instance this introductory section of the poem demonstrates
that he is not so confident as he would have us believe
about the neat causal connection between virtuous labour

and material well-being or about the material and social consequences of his own parochial activities. Furthermore these uncertainties have a damaging effect on what should be his special and secure qualification: his religious commitment.

The poem in fact begins by insisting that *nobody* can hope to prosper in this vale of tears:

> Is there a place, save one the Poet sees,
> A Land of Love, of Liberty and Ease:
> Where labour wearies not nor cares suppress
> Th' eternal flow of Rustic Happiness;
> Where no proud Mansion frowns in aweful State,
> Or keeps the Sunshine from the Cottage-Gate;
> Where Young and Old, intent on pleasure, throng,
> And half man's life, is Holiday and Song?
> Vain search for scenes like these! no view appears,
> By sighs unruffled or unstain'd by tears;
> Since Vice the world subdued and Waters drown'd,
> *Auburn* and *Eden* can no more be found.
>
> (i.15–26)

Crabbe seems to have found a secure — biblical — answer to a question that exercised and confused him in 'The Village'. His vision of rural life is now an historical one but in a thoroughly unhistorical way: nothing has changed or can change after the Fall. But how is this view compatible with the view that the poor can prosper if they are virtuous and work hard? The parson certainly tries to reconcile these views:

> Hence good and evil mix'd, but Man has skill
> And power to part them, when he feels the will;
> Toil, care, and patience bless th' abstemious few,
> Fear, shame, and want the thoughtless herd pursue.

Behold the Cot! where thrives th' industrious Swain,
Source of his pride, his pleasure and his gain;
Screen'd from the Winter's wind, the Sun's last ray
Smiles on the window and prolongs the day.

                                        (i.27–34)

Both of the views put forward here — that nobody can expect to prosper in this world and that the virtuous and hardworking can expect to prosper — are traditional Christian messages to the poor.   But are they compatible with one another?[1]

Clearly, social questions (about the causes and distribution of poverty), ethical questions (about the reasons for virtuous conduct) and metaphysical questions (about the existence of God and a life after death) are intimately connected in the parson's argument.   And before we try to decide whether the parson's two views on poverty and prosperity can in fact be reconciled it is worth clarifying the metaphysical aspect of the problem.

Edmund Leach argued in 'Genesis as Myth' that any 'religious myth' starts by distinguishing this imperfect world from another world which is perfect, everything which this world is not. But religious myth is then faced with the problem of linking these two worlds, finding some mediation between them which will not collapse the distinction between them. Characteristically, Leach argues, such mediation takes the form of anomalous creatures, creatures which belong to both worlds. In Christianity Christ himself is the central mediator, a God-man, the Son of God who lives and dies on earth as a man.[2] The structure of the parson's argument in the introductory section of 'The Parish Register' is directly relevant to these features of religious myth

---

[1] For an alternative reading of Crabbe's argument, see *The Dark Side of the Landscape*, pp.77–88.

[2] *Genesis as Myth and other Essays* (London, 1969), pp.7–23.

as Leach describes it. It is necessary that people, and particularly poor people, should be taught that this world is a vale of tears and that only in another world after death can they hope for contentment. But it is also necessary, if people are to *believe* in the existence of this other world, that some evidence for it should be visibly at work in their present lives in this world. It seems likely then that the two distinct emphases in the parson's argument about poverty are connected to the two requirements of religious myth as Leach describes it. And if the two emphases in the argument about poverty cannot be reconciled the consequences for religious belief itself must be very serious.

It is certainly possible to paraphrase the parson's argument in such a way that his two views on poverty appear complementary rather than contradictory. Thus: 'fallen man must work by the sweat of his brow and expect paradise only in Paradise, but although perfection will not fall into our lap here on Earth virtuous toil does bring some Earthly reward to those who are prepared to work and wait patiently for it'.

Compromise formulations of that kind were a commonplace and the parson may believe he is uttering such a commonplace. But there are features of the lines I have quoted which polarize the two elements of the parson's message so as to bring them into real contradiction. Notably there is a blatant similarity between what the first verse paragraph denies to the common people and what the third verse paragraph confidently offers to those of them who work hard. There is nowhere, the parson insists, where no proud mansion frowns in awful state or keeps the sunshine from the cottage gate; but eleven lines later the same sun is smiling on the window of th' industrious swain's cot. Far from trying to modify the elements of his argument so as to make them consistent the parson seems to be formulating them in a way that is designed to bring them into collision.

A contradiction undoubtedly exists. But identifying the contradiction is not enough; it is just as important to work out what the parson thinks he is doing by describing in such blatantly similar terms what he is withholding and what he is offering. So perhaps we can read the parson's first and third paragraphs as follows: 'Is there a place where no proud mansion keeps the sunshine from the cottage gate? No, there is nowhere where there isn't *some* proud mansion keeping the sun from *some* cottage gate; but there are *some* cottage gates (or is it only cottage windows?) in any place which do get the sun, and these belong to the virtuous toilers'. Different levels of generality can be read into the parson's formulations at different points and the implied triple negative ('no, there is nowhere that has no proud mansions') can seem to add up to a limited kind of positive.

So there are alternative ways of reading the parson's argument. And this is true not only of the first and third verse paragraphs but also of the middle paragraph which offers to link them:

> Hence good and evil mix'd, but Man has skill
> And power to part them, when he feels the will;
> Toil, care, and patience bless th' abstemious few,
> Fear, shame, and want the thoughtless herd pursue.

The second couplet can be read in a number of ways. It can mean that toil, carefulness, abstemiousness and patience keep people from material want while lack of thought for the future results in material want and feelings of fear and shame. This is how I read the couplet when I suggested that, for the parson, people's material circumstances and social status are the consequence of their moral character. But the couplet can also be saying that toil and carefulness and abstemiousness produce a feeling of being blessed while the thoughtless herd suffer the same material deprivation but feel fear and shame as well. Or it could even be saying that I (the parson) bless the virtuous for a toil, abstemiousness and patience whose only other reward is care (in the sense of anxiety), while I find the conduct of the majority who follow their natural desires (their 'wants' as a herd of amoral animals) and live without thought for the morrow (without care) fearsome and shameful.

Is the parson saying that the virtuous poor get the blessing of food and money or only that they get the parson's blessing? Crabbe's use of the word 'bless' is interesting. If parson or poet talk about 'blessings' in the sense of material benefits they are using the word constatively. If the poet uses the word to refer to the parson's calling down of blessings on people he is still using the word constatively but he is referring to a performative use of the word by the parson in his parish work. This is the sense of the word to which he refers at the beginning of the poem when he says he will describe the 'pairs I bless'd in the departed year'. Whether the parson is marrying a couple or administering charity he is engaged in the active allocation of identities to his parishioners. He would like to believe that in identifying people as blessed (rather than cursed) or as deserving (rather than undeserving) he is making a moral distinction which is also an effective social distinction. But the differences between the poet's address to his readers (in which 'blessing' must be constative) and the parson's address to his parishioners (in which it may be performative) enables the parson-poet to avoid being clear about what he is doing to his parishioners.

Radically different meanings of the crucial couplet are all possible. The different available meanings of a number of the words in the couplet allow the lines of cause and effect to be read in different directions. The couplet is an extended and covert pun. The different meanings which it confuses correspond to the views of poverty put forward in the preceding and succeeding verse paragraphs: that virtuous labour leads to material reward and that there is no relation between virtue and material reward. The pun allows parson-poet and reader to travel with scarcely a jolt from one view to another. It enables the parson-poet to present the different views as complementary while admitting, covertly, that they are contradictory.

I have already suggested that the coherence of Christian myth depends directly, in the poem, upon the coherence of the parson's view about poverty. And we can reformulate the connection in a way that suggests parallels with *The Village*. In effect the coherence of the relationship between this world and the next depends upon the coherence of the relationship between two groups of people in this world, the hard-working and the dissolute poor. So the life of the two kinds of poor are supposed to be sub-species of that life-on-Earth which is contrasted with life-after-death. But the need for a link, a mediation, between this world and the other world has the effect of confusing the categorial arrangement. The distinction between the two human groups looks less like a distinction within life-on-Earth and more like a secular reformulation of the distinction *between* life-on-Earth and life-after-death. This is one way of explaining why one of the human groups, the hard workers, seem to enjoy an almost paradisal existence.

But however we formulate the connection between Christian myth and views about poverty, the parson himself is clearly at the centre of the network of relationships involved. He holds all the strings together or he occupies the place where all the strings get tangled. The parson, a human being who is nevertheless God's representative and a special embodiment of the link between this world and the other world, is himself a 'mediating' figure in Leach's sense. The parson with his 'flock' is clearly affiliated to Christ the Shepherd. So if the network of relationships I have described is indeed covertly incoherent, this is an incoherence in the parson's own practice and identity. What, in particular, is the relation between the two kinds of 'blessing' he adminsters?

I have followed the *Complete Poetical Works* in quoting the poem from the second (1808) edition of *Poems*. But in the first (1807) edition Crabbe wrote:

> Such are our Peasants, those to whom we yield
> Glories unsought, the Fathers of the Field;
> And these who take from our reluctant hands,
> What *Burn* advises or the Bench commands.

About one thing the parson is quite clear: he regrets having to administer statutory relief (as ordered by the local magistracy or set down in Burn's *Justice of the Peace*) to the thoughtless herd. These people, he implies, are on the parish as a result of their own laziness and imprudence. They have in effect turned themselves into paupers, joining the traditional pauper class of the sick, aged and mentally disturbed poor. What is not at all clear is what the parson means by the 'Glories unsought' yielded to 'the Fathers of the Field'. The phrase could refer to any one of three things. It could refer to the private (or perhaps parochial) charity willingly given to virtuous toilers, who are not on the parish and do not apply for parish relief. Or, since a parson talking about Glories possibly has heavenly ones in mind, it could refer to the utterance of blessings upon the Fathers of the Field as a reward for the virtuous toil which enables them to live in relative comfort without resort to charity of any kind. Or, thirdly, it could refer to exactly the same kind of statutory relief yielded to the thoughtless herd but given and received in this case in a quite different spirit: given willingly to men who can neither survive on the wages they get from their hard work nor are willing to *ask* for help; who are too proud of their non-existent 'independence' to go to the parish for aid.

Crabbe was evidently worried about these lines or he would not have changed 'Glories unsought' to 'Praise with relief':

> Such are our Peasants, those to whom we yield
> Praise with relief, the Fathers of the Field;

But the alteration only highlights the ambivalence. 'Relief' has to be a pun. In yielding 'Praise with relief' we either call down blessings upon them as we give them their parish relief or we are relieved to be able to praise them for not needing and/or demanding parish aid.

The situation seems to be that hard-working, able-bodied workers cannot generally make ends meet. Need on this scale cannot be met by occasional private charity, only by systematic and general assistance from the rates. A situation of this kind involves a crisis of identity as well as a crisis of subsistence. The reality of patriarchal order is seriously threatened. If assistance is withheld the poor are left completely unprotected from the vicissitudes of a free labour market; if assistance is provided it must be done on a systematic and impersonal scale which removes any quasi-personal element from the relationship between givers and receivers. Whether assistance is provided or withheld the distinction between, for instance, paupers and labourers and the relationship between givers and receivers envisaged by charity are undermined.

The proper context of Crabbe's poem in this respect is the argument about poverty which developed in the 1790s, and the administrative measures adopted in response to that poverty. Particularly relevant are Burke's 1795 essay *Thoughts and Details on Scarcity* and Malthus's 1798 *Essay on the Principle of Population*. Labour, argued Burke, was a commodity like any other commodity bought and sold on the market; it had to find its own level according to the laws of supply and demand. To interfere with this mechanism in the name of any supposed benevolence was to interfere with 'the laws of the market which are the laws of nature and therefore the laws of God'. Institutionalized charity was bad for society and bad for the labourer because it took away the motive for hard work and led people to expect in this world rewards which human beings could only expect in the next world. Judicious private charity was acceptable to Burke because it could distinguish between deserving and undeserving cases and maintain a personal relation between giver and receiver thereby helping to sustain a proper sense of the respective identities and duties of different ranks in society. But Burke suggested that the major part of any ministry to the poor should be the urging upon them of 'patience, labour, sobriety, frugality, and religion'.[3]

Burke's *Reflections on the Revolution in France* (1790) had brilliantly formulated a social order in which things could change in such a way that they remained essentially the same, a society both mobile and stable, in which capitalism developed under the patronage of rather than in conflict with aristocracy. This was a social order based on 'the idea of inheritance' which furnished 'a sure principle of conservation, and a sure principle of transmission; without at all excluding a principle of improvement'; where 'improvement' significantly conflates social advance and increased productivity. A crucial metaphor for and instance of this 'idea of inheritance' is the 'family settlement' or 'entailed' estate, devices which limited the capitalist market so far as *land* was concerned, in the interests of established proprietors.[4]

When, five years later in *Thoughts and Details*, Burke directly faces the problem of poverty he emphasizes some features of patriarchal order (the need for the poor to accept their place, the importance of private charity which sustains people's sense of their place) as a way of rationalizing the rejection of others. The Poor Law, which limits the capitalist market so far as *labour* is concerned, is attacked.

An alternative response to widespread poverty was initiated the year after Burke's essay, in 1796. Subsequently referred to as the Speenhamland system, it extended the Poor Law by offering the poor 'aid-in-wages'; that is, wages were made up to

---

[3] *Thoughts and Details on Scarcity, Originally Presented to the Right Hon. William Pitt, in the month of November, 1795* (London, 1800) pp. 24,3.

[4] Edited by C.C. O'Brien (Harmondsworth, 1968), pp.119–20.

a subsistence level out of the parish poor rate according to a scale calculated on the size of the worker's family and the price of bread. This system (which Crabbe operated in his parish at Muston) was based on certain traditional assumptions. Firstly, it had been assumed that 'the labourer's income was by custom, convention and justice a *living* wage, though a very modest one'.[5] Correlatively, pauperism had been regarded not as a condition to which the poor in general were usually liable but as a phenomenon *sui generis*. Paupers were the old, or sick, or mentally disturbed poor or the orphan child, together with those workers dependent on wage-labour who might be out of work owing to some presumed temporary circumstance such as a bad harvest or a particular change in local opportunities for work. Even though most rural workers and their families in most areas would have been heavily dependent on wage-labour they would not normally have been considered or have considered themselves as elements of an autonomous 'economic' sphere guided by its own laws (Burke's 'laws of the market') and outside the proper scope of state or parochial action.

But while it may be possible to identify two broad tendencies in the discursive and administrative response to the crisis the relationship between theory and practice or intention and result was very confusing indeed. The Speenhamland system in particular had quite unintended results. It was certainly a response based on traditional assumptions and aiming, as Burke also aimed, to maintain an existing social order; but it was a response to an unprecedented situation and had unprecedented and unforeseen consequences. For by committing themselves to making up wages automatically out of the rates the magistrates actually encouraged employers to cut wages even further, thereby forcing more and more able-bodied labourers onto the

---

[5] E. J. Hobsbawm and G. Rudé, *Captain Swing* (London, 1969), p.57; see also K. Polanyi, *Origins of Our Time* (London, 1944).

parish. A measure designed to sustain one of the main distinctions upon which the social order was based — the distinction between labourers and paupers — had the very opposite effect. Parish government was itself undermining the distinctions of status upon which it was based. And if we see these developments in the context of other laws the pattern is even clearer. The Elizabethan laws of Settlement said that only a person who had lived seven years in a parish had a right to continued parish support, thereby making it very difficult for people to move away from their home parish in search of work; and the Combination Acts of 1794 made trade union organization illegal. Taken together these measures meant that the rural worker was being deprived of his traditional status while being denied the opportunity to sell his labour 'freely' in the national market and establish a new kind of identity for himself as a member of a *class*. As Eric Hobsbawm and George Rudé put it, the parish was no longer the fallback but 'the general framework of the labourer's life.'[6]

It is surely these confused social relationships, this confusion of values and identities, to which the parson's lines attest. He is charging one group of poor people with being poor and feckless as a consequence of their own moral weakness, and regretting that they have to be supported; while he is glad to be able to bless the other group who support themselves through hard work. To this extent he is making a distinction between labourers and able-bodied paupers which is also a distinction between the deserving and the undeserving poor. And if 'Glories unsought' and 'Praise with relief' refer to private or parochial charity he is still making more or less the same distinction since this is help given selectively (in cases of temporary hardship or at difficult times of year) to people who are basically self-supporting and do not want or need to regard themselves as dependent paupers. But what the lines covertly admit is that this praiseworthy group

---

[6] *Captain Swing*, p. 47.

may also be dependent on the parish, are also pauperized. The glories and relief then refer to the same kind of aid which is given to the undeserving poor and given for the same reason. In which case the Fathers of the Field are blessed by the parson because they do not expect or demand what in fact they continually need and what is their right according to Speenhamland. In these circumstances the parson would indeed be relieved to be able to praise them because their attitude plays up to an assumption about their status, about the social relations in which they are involved, which the fact of their dependence on the parish makes untenable. If we then look at the various possible readings of the parson's lines together we can see that the distinction between the two social groups, and the conflation of the social distinction with a moral one, is being maintained in a way that covertly subverts it.

There is some evidence that Crabbe was consciously attempting to reconcile different attitudes to the treatment of the poor in 'The Parish Register'. In his essay on 'Crabbe's View of the Poor', W.K. Thomas has argued that the poem is implicitly dedicated to Edmund Burke in an acknowledgement of Burke's patronage which is otherwise strangely absent from Crabbe's work. Thomas argues that the poem's views on poverty are taken directly from Burke's *Thoughts and Details on Scarcity*. The first line of

> Toil, care, and patience bless th' abstemious few,
> Fear, shame, and want the thoughtless herd pursue.

is, Thomas argues, 'the key line of (Crabbe's) moral thesis' and is a transposition into verse of Burke's 'patience, labour, sobriety, frugality and religion' with 'only those changes demanded by the exigencies of metre'.[7]

The reason why Crabbe made his dedication to Burke an

---

[7] *Revue de L'Université D'Ottowa*, p.237.

implicit rather than an explicit one was, according to Thomas, that he also kept a long-standing promise and 'sent the poem to Fox for his perusal'. Burke and Fox were by this time political enemies. Among other things their views on poverty were quite different. Thomas quotes Fox as saying, in the year of Burke's *Scarcity* essay, that 'it is not fitting in a free country that the great body of the people should depend on the charity of the rich'. This is not the language of the Speenhamland magistrates but is consistent with the system named after them. Fox believed that the poor had a right to a living wage or to statutory relief where Burke opposes both rights in the name of the laws of the market and of that selective private charity which could maintain the sort of 'dependent' relationships Fox is attacking.

So far Thomas's argument is convincing. But my own reading of the poem, and of that couplet in particular, would suggest that Crabbe's position is not so clear-cut as Thomas suggests. Crabbe is committed to the view that nobody can expect to avoid poverty and misery in this world but he is also committed to the view that the industrious labourer does win substantial benefits from his labours. His views, in other words, intersect those of Burke and Fox. Everything I have said about the introductory section of 'The Parish Register' suggests that it can be read in a number of different ways — indeed that it has to be readable in a number of different ways in order to give the appearance of being consistent. And my view of the matter is surely supported by the fact that Crabbe did not just 'send the poem to Fox for his perusal'; he sent it to Fox and 'whatever he approved the reader will readily believe that I carefully retained; the parts he disliked are totally expunged'.[8]

---

[8] *The Life of George Crabbe by his Son*, p.175.

Chapter 7

Portraits

If the introductory section of 'Baptisms' is about economic prudence, the rest of 'Baptisms' and the whole of 'Marriages' emphasize the link between economic and sexual prudence. Indeed it is hard to distinguish 'Baptisms' from 'Marriages', to establish the criteria by which stories have been allocated to one rather than to the other. It certainly makes sense to discuss the two books together. Overwhelmingly the stories in both are about sexuality, procreation, marriage, economic management and the connections between these things. We might expect 'Baptisms' to be distinguished by an interest in children but in fact the parson has almost no interest in children in their own right. He is interested in what their arrival in the world tells us about and does to the relationship between their parents. And that interest is what does mark the difference, even though it is not a dramatic or consistent difference, between the two books. Many of the stories in 'Baptisms' focus on the impact of offspring on parental relationships. The difference between wanted and un-

wanted children (whether outside marriage or within it) is taken
as an object lesson (both for us and for the parents) in the consequences of prudence or imprudence. 'Marriages' focuses on
happy and unhappy marriages: marriages which take proper account of the couple's financial circumstances, marriages forced
on couples by the woman's pregnancy.

In other respects the organization of these two books is more
radically unclear. For instance it is often hard to see the connection between the parson's statements about how people ought
to behave — his maxims and homilies — and the stories they
are supposed to introduce or to moralize. And it is often equally
hard to work out the organization of the sequence of contiguous
stories, the logic by which one story leads to another.

'Baptisms' however begins clearly enough in both these respects:

> With evil omen, we that Year begin;
> A Child of Shame, — stern Justice adds, of Sin,
> Is first recorded; — I would hide the deed,
> But vain the wish; I sigh and I proceed:
> And could I well th' instructive truth convey,
> 'Twould warn the Giddy and awake the Gay.
>   (i.277–82)

This first story, of Lucy the Miller's daughter and her sailor
lover, illustrates the misery and shame that follow from having
sex before you get married. If the parson is offering us 'portraits'
this story constitutes a diptych. What breaks Lucy's story in
two, sharply dividing 'before' and 'after', is a sexual relationship
and its immediate aftermath: childbirth and the death of her
lover at sea to which he has returned 'to seek a portion for his
bride'.

The second story represents a clear contrast with the first
one:

> Next with their Boy, a decent Couple came,
> And call'd him *Robert*, 'twas his Father's name;
> Three girls preceded, all by time endear'd,
> And future Births were neither hop'd nor fear'd; ...
> Love all made up of torture and delight,
> Was but mere madness in this Couple's sight: ...
> Few were their Acres, — but with these content,
> They were, each pay-day, ready with their rent;
> (i.403–6, 409–10, 417–18)

and if either Robert or Susan are tempted to small extravagances they 'both — that Waste itself might work in vain —/ Wrought double tides, and all was well again' (431–2). Anything which might threaten radical alteration in their lives is catered for in advance so that their lives may naturally constitute a 'portrait', a single picture, just as the life of Lucy breaks into a diptych. Juxtaposed, the two stories have clear moral implications. One: sexual and economic prudence go hand in hand. Two: prudence leads to contentment and imprudence to misery.

But the relation between story and maxim, and between contiguous stories, is seldom as coherent as this. For one thing there are so many different maxims scattered through 'Baptisms' and 'Marriages', statements of moral principle which it is hard to co-ordinate. A homily on the value of marriage as a controller of unruly passions concludes 'Baptisms' and therefore implicitly introduces 'Marriages'. Then 'Marriages' itself starts with a long statement about the wisdom of 'delay', of not rushing into marriage. 'Yet', the parson concludes, 'not too long in cold Debate remain,/ Till Age, refrain not — but if Old, refrain' (ii.17–18). And 'refrain' is unfortunately the appropriate word because the text of 'Marriages' is punctuated twice by the awful lines: 'Ah! fly temptation, Youth, refrain! refrain!' (ii.129,187) and once by 'Then fly temptation, Youth; resist, refrain!' (ii.245). Surrounded by such a multitude of moral obligations (get married,

delay marriage, don't delay it too long, don't do it at all if you
are old, don't have a sexual relationship before it) what do the
stories themselves manage to say?

The first story in 'Marriages' seems to illustrate the maxim
which immediately precedes it - 'if Old, refrain'. Gaffer Kirk,
ageing but comfortably off, is beguiled into the married state
which he has always scorned by a pretty and craftily submissive
young woman, who, as he soon discovers, only wants him for his
savings. Then,

> 'But had this Tale in other guise been told,'
> Young let the Lover be, the Lady old,
> And that Disparity of Years shall prove
> No bane to Peace, although some bar to Love:
>
> (ii.63–6)

The story that follows illustrates this contention. The young
servant 'blithe *Donald*' from 'the banks of *Tay*' quietly courts
and eventually marries the ageing housekeeper Mistress Dobson.
It is a contented match and in the parson's view a wise one since

> like a Trade-Wind is the Antient Dame,
> Mild to your wish and every day the same; ...
> And then she gently, mildly breathes her last;
> Rich you arrive, in Port awhile remain,
> And for a second Venture sail again.
>
> (ii.75–6, 80–2)

This second story complements the first story as neatly as the
story of Robert and Susan complemented the story of Lucy and
her sailor lover at the beginning of 'Baptisms'. But in doing
so it has made us re-read the story of Gaffer Kirk as a story
not about 'the old' but about relations *between* the old and the
young. The parson introduces that distinction, along with the
distinction between what is proper for men and what is proper
for women, as if he were simply being more specific, introducing

sub-divisions into the category of 'the old'. But of course he is not: his second story contradicts the maxim which indirectly introduced it — 'if Old, refrain'. He is now saying that marriage between a young man and an old woman is fine (if you're a man). Clearly the object of the parson-poet's address has altered too. He appeared to be speaking to all his readers in their capacity as old or potentially old people, but is now speaking man to man.

We are faced with problems of categorization already familiar to us. The parson wants to relate the distinction between right and wrong conduct in the field of marriage to the distinction between youth and age and to the distinction between men and women. He can do this successfully so long as he is talking in very general terms: 'delay a little if you are young, don't get married at all if you are old'. But these dicta do not take specific account of the fact that it takes two people to make a marriage and that they will be of different sexes and may be of very different ages. The stories reveal these obvious facts but, more important, reveal views about the differences between men and women and youth and age in partnership which subvert — where they are intended to refine — the more general category-distinctions.

If the distinction between men and women causes trouble so does the distinction between social classes. Difference of income was clearly important in the first two stories — Gaffer Kirk lost his savings, blithe Donald got the benefit of Mistress Dobson's – but substantial differences of class are more important elsewhere in the poem. The introduction to 'Marriages' broaches the issue:

> If Poor, Delay for future Want prepares
> And eases humble Life of half its Cares;
> If Rich, Delay shall brace the thoughtful Mind,
> T'endure the Ills that ev'n the happiest find:
>
> (ii.5–8)

The logic of the second couplet is rather flimsy, but the real

trouble comes later. After a string of seven unhappy-marriage
stories the parson has an imaginary interlocutor ask:

'But ever frowns your Hymen? Man and Maid,
Are all repenting, suffering or betray'd?'
Forbid it Love! we have our Couples here,
Who hail the Day in each revolving Year:
These are with us, as in the World around;
They are not frequent, but they may be found.
     Our Farmers too, what though they fail to prove,
In Hymen's Bonds, the tenderest Slaves of Love,
(Nor, like those Pairs whom Sentiment unites,
Feel they the fervour of the Mind's Delights;)
Yet coarsely kind and comfortably gay,
They heap the Board and hail the happy Day;
And though the Bride, now freed from School, admits
Of Pride implanted there, some transient fits;
Yet soon she casts her girlish Flights aside,
And in substantial Blessings rests her Pride.
     No more she moves in measured steps; no more
Runs, with bewilder'd ear, her music o'er;
No more recites her French, the Hinds among,
But chides her Maidens in her mother-tongue;
Her Tambour-frame she leaves and Diet spare,
Plain-work and Plenty with her House to share;
Till, all her Varnish lost, in few short years,
In all her Worth, the Farmer's Wife appears.
     Yet not the ancient Kind; nor she who gave
Her Soul to gain — a Mistress and a Slave; ...
But she, the Daughter, boasts a decent Room,
Adorn'd with Carpet, form'd in Wilton's loom;
Fair Prints along the paper'd wall are spread;
There, *Werter* sees the sportive Children fed,
And *Charlotte* here, bewails her Lover dead. ...

Yet not to those alone who bear command,
Heav'n gives a Heart to hail the Marriage Band;
Among their Servants, we the Pairs can show,
Who much to Love and more to Prudence owe:
Reuben and *Rachel* though as fond as Doves,
Were yet discreet and cautious in their Loves;
Nor would attend to *Cupid*'s wild Commands,
Till cool Reflection bade them join their Hands;
When both were poor, they thought it argued ill
Of hasty Love to make them poorer still;
Year after year, with Savings long laid by,
They bought the future Dwelling's full Supply: ...
What if, when *Rachel* gave her Hand, 'twas one
Embrown'd by Winter's Ice and Summer's Sun;
What if, in *Reuben*'s Hair, the female Eye
Usurping Grey among the Black could spy;
What if in both, Life's bloomy Flush was lost,
And their full Autumn felt the mellowing Frost;
Yet Time, who blow'd the Rose of Youth away,
Had left the vigorous Stem without decay;
Like those tall Elms, in Farmer *Frankford*'s Ground,
They'll grow no more, — but all their Growth is sound;
      (ii.384–409, 414–18, 431–42, 449–58)

In the first part of this passage the parson writes as a sociologist, describing what typically happens to the generic farmer's daughter; in the second part he describes a particular case. He juxtaposes, in effect, a 'group' and a 'portrait'. And this raises a problem of proportion: it is hard to tell whether the parson means that happy marriages are normal among those 'who bear command' but rare among 'their Servants'. The problem of proportion is aggravated by the ambiguous use of the term 'Servant' to which reference has been made in a previous chapter: is Crabbe talking about all agricultural employees or only about servants-in-husbandry?

The sequence of the passage is confusing as well. The first verse paragraph, while we read it, seems to refer to the community as a whole. 'These are with us' seems to mean 'these are in our parish'. But the second paragraph begins 'Our Farmers too', as if the first paragraph had been talking not about the parish but about the poorer members of the parish. And then the fourth paragraph begins 'Yet not to those alone who bear command' as if the parson had not already talked about the *lower* ranks.

The parson seems to be having difficulty co-ordinating the fact that he is talking about a single community with the fact that this community is divided into groups. Are the farming class somehow distinct from the community? (Were 'those who farm', in *The Village* distinct from 'the natives of the place'?) Do they regularly find contentment in marriage in a way that is not true of their 'Servants'? In particular, do they really need to delay marriage in the way the introductory section of 'Marriages' suggested? The answer to this last question is surely that they do not. What the farmers' daughters need to do — and generally, it would seem, succeed in doing — is grow out of romantic fantasies learned from Romances; they learn, in effect, *not* to delay. But the parson does nevertheless want to say that the reason for their contentment is essentially the same as the reason for Reuben and Rachel's contentment. All of them are 'prudent':

> Among their Servants, we the Pairs can show,
> Who much to Love and more to Prudence owe:

Both groups can certainly be called prudent in the sense that they learn to cut their romantic coat according to their financial cloth. But for one group this entails delaying marriage and for the other it does not. This contradicts the parson's earlier statement, and the way in which he now uses the word 'Prudence' suggests that he wants to go on having it both ways in this respect. The couplet just quoted can be inflected to suggest either that 'Prudence' applies to both groups or that it applies particularly to the subsequent group, to 'their Servants'. In effect the word 'Prudence' is ambivalent. It can be read either as synonym for 'Delay' or as a more inclusive category of which 'Delay' is one sub-category.

There is however one respect in which both the farmers' daughters and Reuben and Rachel do delay. They delay having sexual relations until they are married. And just as there is a shifting relation of similarity and difference between 'Prudence' and 'Delay' so there is between delaying marriage and delaying sex *until* marriage, and between the terms ('Delay' and 'refrain') normally applied by the parson to these two things. The parson normally uses the word 'Delay' about marriage and 'refrain' about sex, but the possibility of a semantic slide from one to the other is suggested by the fact that on one occasion he uses 'refrain' when he's talking about marriage: 'if Old, refrain', delay for ever.

Delaying marriage and delaying sex until marriage are quite different things, as the case of the farmer's daughters shows (they do the second but not the first). But of course — and as numerous stories in 'Baptisms' and 'Marriages' aim to show — a great cause of hasty, undelayed marriage is undelayed sex. And what the parson seems to do in the course of his poem is covertly confuse the effect with one of its main causes. That this confusion exists is evident if we look at the range of subject-matter treated by the stories. Despite the lengthy sermon on the benefits of delayed marriage there is only one story in 'Baptisms' and only one (the story of Reuben and Rachel) in 'Marriages' about marriages between young people which are happy because they are delayed. There are no stories about marriages which are unhappy because they are not delayed. They are mostly about people who have sex before they are married, some of whom are forced into premature marriage by premature sex. There are no stories at all about young couples who get married in a hurry because they very much want to — about what happens to *them* when they come up against the hardships of housekeeping and offspring. So the long argument for delayed marriage which introduces 'Marriages' has, despite appearances, scarcely any connection with the stories it introduces.

What is the explanation for this curious situation, in which Crabbe makes it appear that he has provided evidence for his argument in favour of delayed marriage but has not actually done so? Part of the answer is that what is in the interest of the parson and ratepayers is not necessarily in the interest of the poor. We have already noticed that 'Prudence' may entail delay for Reuben and Rachel but not for the farmers' daughters. But this double standard may also apply to the poor themselves – Reuben and Rachel notwithstanding. It may be in the interests of the parson and the ratepayers that the poor should delay marriage but not in the interest of the poor themselves. If you marry early you are likely to have more children since you increase the effective period of the wife's fertility. If you are a servant-in-husbandry you are not allowed to marry and you are encouraged to save for an independent household. But if you are a young day-labourer at the height of your earning power there is no such disincentive. Alternatively, if you are a wage-labourer dependent on aid-in-wages from the parish (calculated on the price of bread and the *size of family*) there is no disincentive either: more children may well be bad for the ratepayers but not necessarily bad for the labourer.[1] So we are back with

---

[1] On the issues of class and sexuality involved here see D. Levine, *Family Formation in an Age of Nascent Capitalism* (New York, 1977) and J. Weeks, *Sex, Politics and Society: The regulation of sexuality since 1800* (London and New York, 1981), pp.1–80.

> Toil, care and patience bless th' abstemious few,
> Fear, shame and want the thoughtless herd persue.

This, we recall, says that if you aren't prudent you will suffer but
also says that, though you *ought* to suffer, you probably won't
because we shall be giving you financial assistance. Indeed, two
of the crucially ambiguous words reappear when, at the beginning of 'Marriages', the parson is setting out the reasons for
delayed marriage:

> If Poor, Delay for future Want prepares,
> And eases humble Life of half its Cares;
>
> (ii.5–6)

We are now in a position to notice the evasive vagueness of
these lines. They appear to say that delay will enable you to
save against future hardship (to mitigate future hardship), but
they may only say that delay will teach you to put up with a
hardship which will affect you equally whether you have saved
up or not, whether you are one of 'th' abstemious few' or one of
'the thoughtless herd'.

If this is the case then Reuben and Rachel, the couple whose
delaying and saving do save them from future hardship, are perhaps praised for the same reason that 'the Fathers of the Field'
were praised, to whom, in the introductory section of the poem,
'we' gave 'praise with relief'. That is, the parson is relieved to
find *somebody* who acts as if hard work and prudence could maintain independence even if they may well not do so. These are all
people who behave as if there is a clear distinction between poor
labourers and paupers even though this distinction is scarcely
tenable.

What is involved in such situations is money (the poor would
not lose money by having more children, the ratepayers would);
but also rank, social identity. We have already seen, in the introductory section of the poem, that Crabbe is not as certain as

he wants to appear about the distinctions and relations between one social group and another or about the moral distinctions which he believes coincide with these social distinctions. And if we have another look at the poem's few *happy* marriages we shall see what it is that Crabbe cannot face about marriage among the poor in general. He cannot face the possibility that, from the point of view of the poor themselves, it may not make sense to think about marriage in terms of calculations about their future income, family size, or class position. To think about marriage in these ways might seem very desirable, but it would also seem pointless, an impossible calculation.

The few stories about happy marriages are all about people who know they must marry someone of their own class. In the last story in 'Marriages' Sir Edward Archer loves his bailiff's daughter, Fanny Price. The story ends happily because Sir Edward is realistic and noble enough to realize she would be happier with his rival, a young man who is Fanny's social equal. With Reuben and Rachel and the farmers' daughters the situation is more complex. Like Sir Edward Archer they realize that they should marry within their class. But there is some doubt about just what 'their class' is.

The farmers have enough money and ambition to send their daughters to boarding school but not enough to fulfil the aspirations which this produces in their daughters. The destiny of farmers' daughters is to be hardworking farmers' wives rather than ladies of leisure. This becomes evident to the daughters, who cut their losses and 'the Farmer's Wife appears'. Lower down the social scale, among 'their Servants', Reuben and Rachel delay marriage because

> When both were poor, they thought it argued ill
> Of hasty Love to make them poorer still;

We may conjecture that the similarity of income and social status between their two families would make them natural childhood friends and, ostensibly, ideal marriage partners (their Old Testament names suggest that rules of sectarian endogamy may also be at work). But the same similarity also threatens to make them *un*suitable marriage partners since if they get married, set up their own household and have children both will become poorer than either is while they are single. Because they share exactly the *same* social rank marriage between these two would cause them to *change* their rank, to fall socially; it might pauperize them. So they spend years saving up to get married, to preserve their *present* social position.

Both the farmers' daughters and Reuben and Rachel are faced with an ambiguity about what sort of people it makes sense for them to desire and marry, an ambiguity which arises from their social positions which emit contradictory messages in this respect. The people whom their social position encourages them to think of as marriage partners are very hard to distinguish from the people their social position tells them cannot be marriage partners.

There are four stories of happy marriages in the poem: the farmers' daughters (this is more than one marriage of course), Reuben and Rachel, Fanny Price, and — in 'Baptisms' — Robert and Susan. The story of Fanny Price involves the rejection of marriage across a social frontier: Fanny marries *into* the class she was planning to marry *out* of. The story of Robert and Susan has interesting affinities with the other two, and suggests another dimension to the paradoxical situation faced by Reuben and Rachel and the farmers' daughters:

> *Susan* could think, though not without a sigh,
> If she were gone, who should her place supply;
> And *Robert* half in earnest, half in jest,
> Talk of her Spouse when he should be at rest;
>
> (i.411–14)

Future changes — traumatic loss, new intimacies — are enter-

tained in advance to such an extent that Robert and Susan are
in effect seeing each other as kin: the family they will marry
from as well as the family they have formed by marriage. In a
similar way the relationship between Reuben and Rachel resembles a sibling relationship: an early intimacy which points away
from rather than towards marriage.

What is remarkable is that these paradoxical situations
characterize the *happy* marriages. It is as if it is only there,
where couples *see* themselves faced with almost impossibly
contradictory pressures and can therefore resolve them that
Crabbe can see them either. The sexual life of the poor
in general, in all those relationships which are unhappy or
considered so by the parson, must raise these same issues
but in a way Crabbe cannot or will not recognize. But we
shall be in a better position to understand how this happens when we have examined the place of procreation in the
poem.

The relation between sexuality and marriage is manipulated. Under cover of urging the delay of sex in one respect
(till marriage) the poem urges its double delay (it must be delayed until after a delayed marriage). The relation of sex to
procreation is also manipulated. According to 'The Parish Register' sex before marriage leads to childbirth in every case, but
once a couple are married they can't expect children to arrive
in such an automatic fashion. The message of this inconsis-
tency is that you cannot control the relation between sex and
procreation (unless you are a parson-poet). Children are necessary from the parson's point of view — presumably because
the continuation of the species depends on them, but also because sex must not be indulged in except with the possibility
of childbirth in mind. Nevertheless the parson's fear of the sexual life of the poor manifests itself centrally in a *fear* of children.

The parson has, as I have argued, no interest in children as individuals or in their present relationships with their parents. But this lack of interest is a precondition of the extremely important part they do play in the poem. It is children who, arriving as the consequence of pre-marital sex, ensure that the lives of their parents are broken in two. If the parson is to present his parishioners' lives as pictures in his 'exhibition' (clearly distinguished episodes in his 'annals'), the only alternative to a diptych is a changeless 'portrait'. The story of Robert and Susan has already provided us with an example of how people prevent change, or change only in order to remain the same. The same story illustrates the importance of children in this process. When a new child arrived they 'call'd him *Robert*, 'twas his Father's name'. Of course in any actual parish register this repetition of the Christian name as well as the surname of the father would not be remarkable. But in a poem which scarcely ever tells us the names of the children it is surely significant if, when one *is* named, it has no name of its own.

Children arrive into an existing relationship. But they arrive, paradoxically, from inside the relationship. Children are therefore, for the parson-poet, anomalous creatures who always threaten to disturb a clear distinction between categories. For the parson-poet the arrival of children must either destroy the parental relationship (making it radically other than itself) or disappear back into the adult relationship (be the same as its parents who thereby remain the same). The relation between parents and *parson* must be, in the parish, a very close one. They christen the child together and if a household cannot live 'independently' (from rents, from working their own land, from state office, from wages) the parish becomes their household, as it does more directly for the orphaned apprentice. The parson acting for the parish is indeed a kind of 'father' in such cases.

The tensions involved in the relationship between the parson and the parish came out most clearly, as we should by now expect, in a story in which those tensions are resolved:

> To name an Infant met our Village-sires,
> Assembled all, as such event requires; ...
> Some harden'd knaves, who rov'd the country round,
> Had left a Babe within the Parish-bound. — ...
> Then by what name th' unwelcome guest to call,
> Was long a question and it posed them all:
> For he who lent it to a Babe unknown,
> Censorious men might take it for his own;
> They look'd about, they gravely spoke to all,
> and not one *Richard* answer'd to the call;
> Next they enquir'd the day, when passing by,
> Th' *unlucky* peasant heard the stranger's cry; ...
> At last with all their words and work content,
> Back to their homes, the prudent Vestry went,
> And *Richard Monday* to the Workhouse sent.
>   (i.688–9, 692–3, 698–705, 708–10)

Robert's name absorbed him completely in his father's identity: he only had a surname. Richard Monday's name is designed to show who is *not* his father: he has two 'given' names and no real surname.

If the parson is not interested in children as characters in their own right, Richard Monday is the exception which proves the rule since he has no character at all:

> Patient in all controul, in all abuse,
> He found contempt and kicking have their use:
> Sad, silent, supple; bending to the blow,
> A slave of slaves, the lowest of the low;
> His pliant soul gave way to all things base,
> He knew no shame,he dreaded no disgrace:
> It seem'd, so well his passions he suppress'd,
> No feeling stirr'd his ever-torpid breast;
> Him might the meanest pauper bruise and cheat,
> He was a foot-stool for the beggar's feet;

His were the legs that ran at all commands;
They us'd on all occasions, *Richard*'s hands;
His very soul was not his own; he stole
As others order'd, and without a dole;
In all disputes, on either part he lied,
And freely pledg'd his oath on either side;
In all rebellions *Richard* join'd the rest,
In all detections *Richard* first confess'd;
Yet though disgrac'd, he watch'd his time so well,
He rose in favour, when in fame he fell;
Base was his usage, vile his whole employ,
And all despis'd and fed the pliant boy:

(i.713–34)

The ambivalence of the relationship between Richard and his adoptive parish is captured at the start of the story in the parson's descripton of the parish vestry (of which he, despite his satirical tone, would be a member) as the 'Village-sires'. The word 'sire' means both biological father and king or lord. The word's double sense marks very precisely the patriarchal character of the social order in which the parson is involved. The parish takes on numerous quasi-familial obligations. It is governed by a vestry, its political sires who are also heads of households and frequently fathers, biological sires. In the case of Richard Monday the proximity between the different levels of patriarchal authority theatens to undermine the distinction between those levels, where sires might be mistaken for sires, where the *in loco* part of *in loco parentis* threatens to disappear. He and the parish sires are almost, like Robert and Susan, kin *and* not-kin. And just as their name for him adopts him and rejects him, marking him as not-theirs, so their enslavement of him enables them to alienate into him all those tasks and features upon which they depend and which they do not want to acknowledge as their own. An orphan foundling without a name he is an obligation upon, and then a necessity to, the parish which is his family and his prison. Richard is cast by fortune into a frowning parish. He comes into this almost closed world from outside but they must accept him because he is found inside the parish, 'within the Parish-bound'. He is a borderline case.

In this story the activity of the parson when he christens babies directly meets the activity of the poet when he invents and names characters. We first read the boy's name in the following couplet:

> Back to their homes, the prudent Vestry went,
> And *Richard Monday* to the Workhouse sent.

It is as if the vestry have invented him, launched a fictional character into real life. Richard's life has the structure of a Life:

> Now *Richard*'s talents for the world were fit,
> He'd no small cunning and had some small wit; ...
> Steel, through opposing plates the Magnet draws,
> And steelly atoms culls from dust and straws;
> And thus our Hero, to his interest true,
> Gold through all bars and from each trifle drew;
> But still more surely round the world to go,
> This Fortune's Child, had neither friend nor foe.
> Long lost to us, at last our man we trace,
> Sir *Richard Monday* died at *Monday-place*;
>
> (i.741-2, 747-54)

The term "Hero' is in one sense ironic since Richard is the opposite of heroic. But this is also a double irony, or no irony at all, since Richard's life is indeed a deliberately contrived invention, a 'plot' in both senses, first on the part of the people who leave him in the parish, then on the part of the parish who name and use him, then on the part of Richard himself making the vestry's invention his own, then on the part of the state which eventually renames him Sir Richard Monday. And finally on the part of the author in his capacity both as parson and as poet. When the parson-poet writes 'Long lost to us, at last our man we trace', the word 'trace' means both to discover and to inscribe. And 'our' refers not only to the parish but also the poet and his readers. Richard Monday does not appear in 'Burials' because of course he dies in another parish; but it is as if the parson-poet has 'traced' (written and then read) his name as he looks through the parish's filing cabinet, the Register from which Richard Monday, whose name very much created him, was 'long lost'.

Crabbe's treatment of sexuality, marriage and the production of offspring are all of a piece. These activities must continue if the human race is to continue; but they must be carried on in such a way that the alterations of identity they involve are kept to an absolute minimum. If you can change in such a way that you remain the same you appear as a 'portrait' in the gallery of human existence. Any more substantial alteration in a couple's relationship must break it into separate pieces so that your Life takes the form of a before-and-after dyptich. The maintenance of the belief that life has the structure of a formal representation comes to depend, in 'The Parish Register', on this radical polarization of sameness and difference in the conduct of the relationship between the sexes.

Certain features of this polarization might lead us to a psychoanalytical explanation of it. A shifty use of the words 'refrain' and 'Delay' helps to disguise a double limitation on sexual activity as a single limitation. A covert fear of sexuality is revealed through a punning process. The implication would be that sexual desire, for Crabbe (for the parson-poet?) is forbidden because it is incestuous. And this seems relevant to the poem if we then remember that incestuous desire is desire for the same, for our own kin(d). The problem is that a psychoanalytic account of sameness and difference leaves out of account other factors which are at least equally important in the poem.

In my view anthropological concepts are more capable of co-ordinating the various factors involved.[2] Anthropological discussions of kinship and marriage distinguish between rules which require a person to marry one of their own kind — rules of endogamy — and rules which require a person to marry someone of a different kind — rules of exogamy. Most societies have strong rules of both kinds, operating at different levels but necessarily affecting each other. All societies have rules forbidding people to marry some of the people to whom they are close kin. At the level of kin one must marry someone of a different kind. But most societies also have rules of endogamy which *require* that a person marries someone of the same kind as themselves at the level of rank or race or nation. There are of course numerous possibilities, with endogamy and exogamy operating at each level. Difficulties in the practice of these rules will occur at each level and between the levels. My reading of 'The Parish Register' suggests that the poem articulates difficulties of this kind, difficulties which may have a quite precise historical location.

Crabbe (Hazlitt's 'Malthus turned metrical romancer') is haunted by the fear, a fear provoked mainly by the sexual conduct of the parish poor, that sameness and difference are indistinguishable, that it may be impossible to distinguish between those you should marry and those you should not marry. The world, he fears, is overwhelmingly made up of situations which are neither like portraits nor like sequences of portraits (narratives) but are intolerable combinations, transitional states in which A and not-A cannot be distinguished.

What are the reasons for believing that the poem articulates fears and difficulties of this kind? In the first place, as we have seen, the poem disguises a double limitation on sex as a single one: this suggests a tension between the conviction that sexual-

---

[2] See especially E. Leach, *Social Anthropology* (London, 1982), pp.149–211.

ity and procreation must go on and a belief that they must not go on. Secondly, as we have seen, the difficulties which the minority of happy families overcome are not mentioned as factors which defeat the majority. The majority are unhappy for *moral* reasons; so the parson would have us and them believe. They fail to exercise sexual and economic prudence. But it is surely proper to assume that they are in fact overwhelmed by the difficulties which the minority recognize and overcome. These difficulties have to do, more or less explicitly, with rules of endogamy and exogamy, at the level of class and at the level of kin. The successful minority marry people of the same kind in terms of class, but this is not an easy task. It may be difficult for them to know what their own class is (the farmers' daughters have been educated as young ladies); or marrying someone of their own class may undermine the class of both individuals unless they save for a long time (the case of Reuben and Rachel). Furthermore marrying someone of the same kind in terms of class seems almost to necessitate marrying someone of the same kind in terms of kin (which is of course forbidden).

If you are a wage-labourer — rather than a farm servant — there is no material incentive to marry late and delay childbirth. If you are a wage-labourer whose low wages will be supplemented according to the price of bread and the number of your children there is no incentive either. What is more it would be impossible, even if it seemed desirable, to make careful calculations about who or when you should marry in terms of your future material circumstances or status. But the opposite is the case for the parson and ratepayers whose quasi-family these offspring become. It does not matter if the farmers' daughters marry early so long as they redirect their attentions towards young farmers as they apparently do: their children will not become a burden on the parish. Crabbe's moralism is directed towards the poor. And he is not simply telling them to behave. He is trying to reconstitute as a moral imperative, through the administrative and linguistic devices available to him, a sense of reciprocally defined identities in a predictable community life at the same time as he colludes in undermining the material supports of that moral imperative. Whether he succeeded in blessing and cursing the poor into better behaviour seems doubtful. They clearly frighten him, even into a sense that, if the community is a kind of family (and he the quasi-father) desire itself may be impossible.

Chapter 8

Death and Narrative

> When these my Records I reflecting read,
> And find what Ills these numerous Births succeed;
> What powerful Griefs these Nuptial Ties attend,
> With what regret these painful Journeys end;
> When from the Cradle to the Grave I look,
> Mine I conceive a melancholy Book.
>
> (iii.17–22)

The idea of life as a journey from the cradle to the grave is an old one. Here it is associated with the space between the Baptisms and the Burials sections of the Parish Register and 'The Parish Register'. Existence finds its truth in this narrative sequence, these 'simple Annals'.

This conflation of life and narrative has been criticised. Louis Mink for instance argues that

> Stories are not lived but told. Life has no begin-
> nings, middles, or ends; there are meetings, but

the start of an affair belongs to the story we tell
ourselves later. ... Only in the story is it America
which Columbus discovers... [1]

Crabbe's poem suggests that Mink is partly wrong and partly
right. He is wrong because baptisms and marriages and funerals
divide people's lives into segments and link the segments together
sequentially. They turn existences into stories with beginnings,
middles and ends. They are rituals which take place in real life,
giving babies identities and turning daughters into wives; they
are not things which are 'told' rather than 'lived' even though
they involve language, naming, the whole apparatus of narra-
tion. But Mink is also right insofar as these are cultural rather
than natural processes: it is the cultural organization of birth
and coupling and death into baptism and marriage and funeral
which in Christian cultures helps to construct our lives as narratives. He is right too to imply that deception and the operations
of power are intrinsic to these cultural processes. If Columbus invented rather than discovered America the trick worked because
Europeans were more powerful than the people they succeeded in
calling 'Indians'. And we have seen similar operations of power
at work in 'The Parish Register' where the parson-poet, sometimes in his capacity as parson and sometimes in his capacity as
poet, manipulates his parishioners' lives more than he cares to
admit. Any narrative (any semiotic process for that matter) involves a double movement: the separation of a whole into parts
and the linking of the parts. Crabbe insists that people must see
their lives either as 'portraits' — existences where things change
only that they remain the same — or as diptychs, juxtaposed
portraits linked by an ironic logic.

But where death is concerned the relation between existence
and narrative changes somewhat. Alasdair MacIntyre, replying

---

[1] 'History and Fiction as Modes of Comprehension', *New Literary
History*, 1 (1970), pp.541–58 (pp.557–8).

to Mink's contention that 'Life has no beginnings, middles, or ends', writes:

> Certainly we must agree that it is only retrospec-
> tively that hopes can be characterized as unfulfilled
> or battles as decisive and so on. But ... to some-
> one who says that in life there are no endings, or
> that final partings take place only in stories, one
> is tempted to reply, 'But have you never heard of
> death?'[2]

In other words there is a very special relation between narrative and death. Both for the dying and for the witnesses of death it can represent an undeniable End. It can lead people to see their whole lives retrospectively, in the form of a story. In his essay on Nikolai Leskov, 'The Storyteller', Walter Benjamin described this special relationship between narrative and death:

> It is ... characteristic that not only a man's knowl-
> edge of wisdom, but above all his real life — and
> this is the stuff that stories are made of — first
> assumes transmissible form at the moment of his
> death. Just as the sequence of images is set in mo-
> tion inside a man as his life comes to an end —
> unfolding the views of himself under which he has
> encountered himself without being aware of it —
> suddenly in his expressions and looks the unfor-
> gettable emerges and imparts to everything that
> concerned him that authority which even the poor-
> est wretch in dying possesses for the living around
> him. This authority is at the very source of the
> story.[3]

---

[2] *After Virtue*, p.197.

[3] *Illuminations*, edited by H. Arendt (London, 1970) pp.83–109 (p.94).

The quality of the stories in 'Burials' springs from the special relationship between narrative and death which MacIntyre and Benjamin begin to define for us. For one thing there is often less evidence of manipulation — by parson or poet — in the presentation of people's lives as exemplary narratives. Perhaps people are — as Benjamin suggests — enabled to see their own lives in this way by the imminence of death: no legal-theological intervention is required. This is one aspect of the 'authority' to which Benjamin refers. Another is that the dying are undergoing an experience which all of us — including the parson — will undergo but which — unlike baptism and marriage — none of us have yet undergone.

The lives of the dying are naturally exemplary without interference by the parson or the particular cultural rules and regulations of which he is a part. They seem of their own accord to constitute themselves as exemplary stories. But for this very reason the nature of the moral lesson which they exemplify may be far less clear than in other cases. It is, admittedly, easier for the parson to show that the inevitable consequence of life is death than it is for him to show that the inevitable consequence of sloth is poverty or of sex before marriage is childbirth and misery. But he can at least *show* us the miseries of unhappy marriages and unmarried mothers; he cannot show us the happiness of Heaven or the misery of Hell. Insofar as death is an End each story can indeed remind us of the vanity of human wishes. But there is a looseness of shape and an uncertainty of moral implication about the stories because although from one point of view death is indeed an End, from another point of view — a Christian point of view — it is also a middle or a beginning.

Dante claimed to share and show the perspective from after death, describing the consequences in Hell and Purgatory and Heaven of the earthly lives lived by people he knew. He could present the kind of poetic justice which Crabbe can present in 'Baptisms' and 'Marriages'. Crabbe is a Christian poet too, but

not a medieval one. He can judge people in this life and use
his pastoral, political, and literary position in an attempt to
enforce those judgements. But as people approach death (losing
the capacity for sex or hard work) the obligation to moralize
their lives may have to compromise with or be superseded by
the obligation to withhold judgement. It is really only God who,
for the Christian, can see these lives in perspective and know
what will constitute poetic justice in their case.

So the parson is acting under a variety of possibly conflicting
pressures as he writes these stories about the dead and dying.
We can see some of these pressures at work already in the story of
the 'rustic infidel' in 'Baptisms': 'Last in my List, five untaught
Lads appear;/ Their Father dead, Compassion sent them here'/
(i.787–8). It is the life and death of the father which really
interests the parson. The man is a loner, atheist, believer in free
love, who calls 'the Wants of Rogues the Rights of Man' (i.815).
The tone is confidently critical and satirical, until the final lines:

> By night as business urg'd, he sought the Wood,
> The ditch was deep, the rain had caus'd a flood;
> The foot-bridge fail'd, he plung'd beneath the Deep,
> And slept, if truth were his, th'eternal sleep.
>
> (i.820–3)

What is the implication, the tone, of the last line? Literally
it means that if the atheist is right in believing there is no life
after death then permanent extinction is the man's fate. And
the implication seems to be that this would represent a kind of
poetic justice which would, paradoxically, vindicate the Christian author. Perhaps the idea that accident finally causes the
rationalist's come-uppance is involved. But then the man never
claimed he would live forever so where is the irony really? Is the
parson simply pleased that the man is dead? In any case these
are cheap bar-room ironies because presumably the parson does
not believe that the man is extinct. In which case perhaps the

tone of the line is one of genuine puzzlement, in the face of a life
whose moral logic he cannot figure out. In which case a properly Christian refusal to judge the dead (to say whether they are
saved or damned) merges into a deeper scepticism. Since there is
no evidence in the man's mode of living or dying for the secular
efficacy of Christian belief — he doesn't seem to have suffered,
in his own eyes, as a consequence of his beliefs — there is a sense
in which the parson himself is challenged in *his* beliefs. 'If truth
were his' can be read as a serious conditional clause rather than
a rhetorical one, and the parson becomes an agnostic. So we
can read the line in a number of tones of voice, give it various
implications, none of which can be relied upon.

After a life which advertised self-confidence and self-
direction the man dies suddenly, a victim of circumstances beyond his control. Crabbe is very interested in the suddenness
of death, but it is often suddenness of a special kind. Of
the publican Andrew Collett (the first entry in 'Burials') he
asks:

> On Death like his what name shall we bestow,
> So very sudden! yet so very slow?
> 'Twas slow: — Disease augmenting year by year,
> Show'd the grim King by gradual steps brought near:
> 'Twas not less sudden; — in the night he died,
> He drank, he swore, he jested and he lied;
> Thus aiding Folly with departing Breath: —
> 'Beware *Lorenzo*, the slow-sudden Death.'
>
> (iii.117–24)

Slow-suddenness is not peculiar to death. In a sermon on 'The
Worth of the Soul', Crabbe wrote:

> First, he thinks his sins few and little. Is it not a
> little one? And then he fancies there is no danger
> in committing them, and so he grows secure, and

commits greater, and thus infallibly acquires the
habit of sin, and generally falls from one step to
a lower and lower still. Our soul's enemy would
persuade us, just as we would persuade ourselves
— he always insinuates into our minds. 'Where
is the danger?' 'Where is the hazard?' 'Will God
condemn you for such pardonable light offences?'
... 'Indulge! indulge! O man' ... Thus reasons
our souls enemy, or thus persuade our desires and
passions, our sense, our companions, or our opportunities, and so men yield and become con-
firmed in the habit of disobedience, and are finally
lost.

Arthur Pollard, who quotes this 'description of a sinner's
progress' points out that it describes 'a basic pattern of many individual downfalls which Crabbe's tales portray'.[4] Sexual temptation is of course a major case in point; in the life of Lucy
Collins for instance whose progress from giving her attention to
the sailor to 'giving her ALL' is an example of just this slow-
sudden pattern. The sinner's progress shows very clearly how
one condition can be suddenly, by its own internal logic, transformed into another, so that a life is broken into two juxtaposed
frames. Correlatively the lives that remain unbroken portraits
are those in which more or less all temptation is avoided from the
start, all inevitable change is forseen and allowed for in advance.
It could be said of course that death cannot be neutralized or
contained in this way. But it's worth remembering that one thing
Robert and Susan did was precisely to foresee the possibility of
their own and their partner's death and build that possibility
into the sober restraint of their present relationship.

But there were not many people in 'Baptisms' or 'Marriages'
like that, and in 'Burials':

---

[4] *English Sermons* (London, 1963), pp.37–8.

Where now is perfect Resignation seen?
Alas! it is not on the Village-Green, —
I've seldom known, though I have often read
Of, happy Peasants on their Dying-bed;
Whose Looks proclaim'd that Sunshine of the Breast,
That more than Hope, that Heav'n itself express'd.
   What I behold are feverish fits of Strife,
'Twixt fears of Dying and desire of Life;
Those earthly Hopes, that to the last endure;
Those Fears, that Hopes superior fail to cure;
At best a sad submission to the Doom,
Which, turning from the Danger, lets it come.
                                   (iii.23–34)

For instance:

Next died the Widow *Goe*, an active Dame,
Fam'd, ten miles round, and worthy all her Fame;
She lost her Husband when their Loves were young,
But kept her Farm, her Credit and her Tongue: ...
No Parish-Business in the Place could stir,
Without Direction or Assent from her;
In turn she took each Office as it fell;
Knew all their Duties and discharg'd them well; ...
   Thus long she reign'd, admir'd, if not approv'd;
Prais'd, if not honour'd; fear'd, if not belov'd; —
When, as the busy Days of Spring drew near,
That call'd for all the Forecast of the Year;
When lively Hope the rising Crops survey'd,
And April promis'd what September pay'd;
When stray'd her Lambs where *Gorse* and
                              Greenweed grow;
When rose her Grass in richer Vales below;
When pleas'd she look'd on all the smiling Land,
And view'd the Hinds, who wrought at her command,

(Poultry in groups still follow'd where she went;)
Then, Dread o'ercame her, — that her Days were spent.
 'Bless me! I die and not a Warning giv'n, —
With *much* to do on Earth and ALL for heav'n!
No Reparation for my Soul's Affairs,
No Leave petition'd for the Barn's Repairs;
Accounts perplex'd, my Interest yet unpaid,
My Mind unsettled and my Will unmade; —
A Lawyer haste, and in your way, a Priest;
And let me die in one good Work at least.'
She spake and, trembling, dropp'd upon her knees,
Heaven in her Eye and in her Hand her Keys:
And still the more she found her Life decay,
With greater force she grasp'd those Signs of Sway:
Then fell and died! ... In haste her Sons drew near,
And dropp'd, in haste, the tributary Tear,
Then from th'adhering Clasp the Keys unbound,
And Consolation for their Sorrows, found.
                    (iii.125–8, 139–42, 163–90)

One of the insights in this splendid passage is indeed an insight
into tempo. John Berger has suggested that when people become aware of their approaching death 'the notion of repetition
is suddenly removed from the reality of time'.[5] This alteration
in the experience of time is captured very powerfully in these
lines partly because it is *not* registered by any explicit change of
grammatical tense. The verbal form in which specific past events
are described (of 'Then Dread o'ercame her', of 'She spake and,
trembling, dropp'd upon her knees', of 'Then fell and died') is
the same as the verbal form in which the habitual activities of
her previous life are described. This gives a particular pathos
to the lines in which the season of her death is described (the

---

[5] *A Fortunate Man: the story of a country doctor* (London, 1967),
p.116.

lines beginning 'When, as the busy Days of Spring drew near'). They emphasize the habitual, repetitive character of her life in the repetitious events of the agricultural year; but these events also require to be read — as she is suddenly having to read them — as unique and unrepeatable and irreversible events so far as she is concerned. The agricultural year and the parish year keep different time from the life of any one participant in them. And the sudden awareness of that difference is greatest for a person like her who has been in command of the operations of farm and parish.

The Widow's is a vivid example of the kind of death with which the parson is most familiar, of those who end their lives ''Twixt fears of Dying and desire of Life' (iii.30). A woman who seemed to have a very secure title to the land of the living suddenly finds herself a stranger in it, a native neither of this world nor another. It is a woman similarly stranded who is the subject of the longest 'portrait' in 'The Parish Register'. As a prototype for the longer stories which Crabbe started to publish three years later in *The Borough*, it is worth examining in some detail.

> Down by the Church-way-Walk and where the Brook
> Winds round the Chancel like a Shepherd's Crook:
> In that small House, with those green Pales before,
> Where Jasmine trails on either side the Door;
> Where those dark Shrubs that now grow wild at will,
> Were clipt in form and tantaliz'd with skill;
> Where Cockles blanch'd and Pebbles neatly spread,
> Form'd shining Borders for the Larkspurs' Bed; —
> There liv'd a *Lady*, wise, austere and nice,
> Who shew'd her Virtue by her Scorn of Vice;
> In the dear Fashions of her Youth she dress'd,
> A pea-green *Joseph* was her favourite Vest;
> Erect she stood, she walk'd with stately Mien,

Tight was her length of Stays and she was tall and lean.
　There long she liv'd in Maiden-state immur'd,
From Looks of Love and treacherous Man secur'd;
Though Evil-frame — (but that was long before)
Had blown her dubious Blast at *Catherine*'s Door:
A Captain thither, rich from *India* came,
And though a Cousin call'd, it touch'd her Fame;
Her annual Stipend rose from his Behest,
And all the long-priz'd Treasures, she possess'd: —
If aught like Joy a while appear'd to stay,
In that stern Face and chase those Frowns away;
'Twas when her Treasures she dispos'd for view,
And heard the Praises, to their Splendour due;
Silks beyond Price, so rich they'd stand alone,
And Diamonds blazing on the buckled Zone;
Rows of rare Pearls by curious Workmen set,
And Bracelets fair in Box of glossy Jet;
Bright polish'd Amber precious from its Size,
Or Forms, the fairest Fancy could devise;
Her Draw'rs of Cedar shut with secret Springs,
Conceal'd the Watch of Gold and rubied Rings;
Letters, Long Proofs of Love and Verses fine
Round the pink'd Rims of crisped Valentine.
Her China Closet, cause of daily Care,
For Woman's Wonder held her pencill'd Ware;
That pictur'd Wealth of *China* and *Japan*,
Like its cold Mistress, shunn'd the Eye of Man.
　Her neat small Room, adorn'd with Maiden-taste,
A clipt French-Puppey first of Favourites grac'd.
A Parrot next, but dead and stuff'd with Art;
(For Poll, when living, lost the Lady's Heart,
And then his Life; for he was heard to speak
Such frightful Words as ting'd his Lady's Cheek;)
Unhappy Bird! who had no power to prove,

Save by such Speech, his Gratitude and Love.
A grey old Cat his Whiskers lick'd beside;
A type of Sadness in the House of Pride.
The polish'd Surface of an India-Chest,
A glassy Globe, in Frame of Ivory, prest;
Where swam two finny Creatures; one of Gold,
Of Silver one; both beauteous to behold:
All these were form'd the guiding Taste to suit:
The Beasts well-manner'd and the Fishes mute:
A widow'd *Aunt* was there, compell'd by Need,
The Nymph to flatter and her Tribe to feed;
Who, veiling well her Scorn, endur'd the Clog,
Mute as the Fish and fawning as the Dog.
   As years increas'd, these Treasures her Delight,
Arose in Value in their Owner's sight: —
A Miser knows that, view it as he will,
A Guinea kept is but a Guinea still:
And so he puts it to its proper Use,
That something more this Guinea may produce:
But Silks and Rings in the Possessor's Eyes,
The oft'ner seen, the more in Value rise,
And thus are wisely hoarded to bestow,
The kind of Pleasure that with years will grow.
But what avail'd their Worth, — if Worth had they, —
In the sad Summer of her slow Decay?
   Then we beheld her turn an anxious Look
From Trunks and Chests and fix it on her Book;
A rich-bound Book of Prayer the Captain gave,
(Some Princess had it, or was said to have,)
And then once more on all her Stores, look round
And draw a sigh so piteous and profound,
That told, 'Alas! how hard from these to part,
And for new Hopes and Habits form the Heart!
What shall I do (she cried) my Peace of Mind,

To gain in dying and to die resign'd?'
   'Hear,' we return'd; — 'these Bawbles cast aside,
Nor give thy GOD a Rival in thy Pride;
Thy Closets shut and ope thy Kitchen's Door;
There own thy Failings, *here* invite the Poor;
A friend of *Mammon* let thy Bounty make,
For Widows' Prayers, thy Vanities forsake;
And let the Hungry of thy Pride, partake:
Then shall thy inward Eye with joy survey,
The Angel *Mercy* tempering *Death*'s Delay!'
   Alas 'twas hard; the Treasures still had Charms,
Hope still its Flattery, Sickness its Alarms;
Still was the same unsettled, clouded View,
And the same plaintive Cry, 'What shall I do?'
   Nor Change appear'd: for, when her Race was run,
Doubtful we all exclaim'd, 'What has been done?'
Apart she liv'd and still she lies alone;
Yon earthy Heap awaits the flattering Stone,
On which Invention shall be long employ'd
To shew the various Worth of *Catherine Lloyd.*
                     (iii.312–412)

We start with the remnants of the Lady's life — her house and now overgrown garden — and end with the official monument to it, her gravestone. In between, the movement of attention is roughly as follows. We move from the present state of her house and garden to its state when she was alive and from there to a description of the Lady herself in those outward appearances through which she was alone known. We then move backwards again in time, searching for the relationships, events, and feelings to which the appearances seem to point as if to their own origin. Defeated in this attempt to move inwards by moving backwards we move forward again in time: in time with her own life as she moves slowly, and at length suddenly, towards her death. Finally we move forward beyond her death to her gravestone on which it will be hard to decide what to inscribe.

The story is a seamless garment of signs: signs which, by virtue of their being signs, point beyond themselves to a truth which will be what the signs signify, which will finally explain all the signifying details. But these seem to be self-defeating signs. The attempt to pass from sign to thing, to get to find the insides which these outsides announce, is continually frustrated. That is why we have to move backwards and forwards over an unbroken surface of signs which always only lead us to other signs. We start with her overgrown cottage, a sign of her absence from it, and though that leads us back to her presence in it, her presence itself appears as a whole series of signs of absence. We end up at her gravestone which is of course itself a sign of absence.

The story puts parson, poet, reader, and finally Catherine herself, together as readers of signs, as people engaged in an attempt to establish a true story. But the problems experienced in doing that, the invitation to do so and the obstacles to doing so, are laid at the door of Catherine Lloyd. The particular character of her life is the cause of our wanting to tell and being unable to tell her Life. Her life is represented as an incitement to us to interpret the clues which she offers about herself and simultaneously as a refusal to let us do so. Inside her house she is doubly protected: 'in Maiden-state immur'd'; 'she shew'd her Virtue by her Scorn of Vice'; 'In the dear Fashions of her Youth she dress'd'. She surrounds herself with possessions which seem to speak, indirectly, of her because they seem to speak of their own past. The 'Rows of Pearls by curious Workmen set' are, like her other possessions, ventriloquists' dummies. They have value for her and a fascination for us because they speak of the possible captain who may possibly have given them to her and of the workmen whose labour is evident in them. But they speak of the absence of these people and relationships and activities, which have in effect disappeared *into* these signs of them so that the physical possessions themselves have the congealed life of fetishes, of corpses. The wonderfully 'mute' fish is unnerving because it is the remains of something which never spoke anyway since fishes don't speak. The Lady's scorn of vice speaks of a virtue which may be its complement but which may not exist at all except as the scorn of vice which offers to speak of it. Catherine's existence puts us in a double-bind, simultaneously inviting us in and closing the door. On the other hand she is — and this is what happens as she becomes aware of her approaching death — the victim of this double-bind. She finds herself trapped by the present, by surfaces, by signs which she now experiences as being no more than that. They cease to be signs because they have become no more than signs of their own status as signs, like the Widow Goe's keys.

The parson-poet's own attitude to her is also a double, ambivalent one. From one point of view his message is that Catherine's virtues consist precisely and only in her scorn of vice, that there is nothing behind that. Catherine Lloyd as she is at the end, surrounded by dross, caught twixt fears of dying and desire of life, is the truth about Catherine Lloyd, at least about her as she now is. From this point of view the final lines of the story are omnisciently ironic: there *is* nothing to say about Catherine Lloyd, whose whole life has been a finally successful attempt to disappear into her remains.

But we can also read the final lines of the story as quite unironic. Crabbe may be saying that there is indeed lots that could be said about Catherine Lloyd if only we could discover it, which we can't. If the first reading implies a wholly secular, even atheistical, attitude on the parson's part this second reading could imply a Christian one (though it need not do so). On this second reading the implication would be that it is indeed possible to read the signs, to travel backwards and inwards from them to a reality (her soul perhaps) which can in principle be known, but could only in practice be known by a God, not from any perspective available to us in this world. Of course such a God would not have to read signs since he would see immediately into the reality of souls or human relationships. But at least from his perspective what must remain for us cryptic and dispersed signs would all fall into place, into perspective, so that the Life of Catherine Lloyd could indeed be told.

The treatment of her name is perhaps significant in this context. We do not in fact learn her full name until the end: '*Catherine Lloyd*' are the last two words of the story. It is as if we travel, in the course of the poem, from a condition of uncertainty in which we do not know who this woman is, to a condition of final knowledge in which her identity is revealed. But this name appears only after she is dead, as the name of an absence; as a name which draws attention to the fact that while proper names are proper to people, the necessary and visible signs of their identity, they are also as arbitrary as any other sign.

The final effect of the story is of Crabbe caught between different views of Catherine Lloyd. The final effect of her name is to suggest the difficulty of getting beyond its material existence as a signifier. Printed in italics it is very much a written name: the name chiselled on her gravestone, the name written by the parson in his register, the name written by the poet at the end of his story, the name printed by the printer.

It could be said that we are all — parson and poet and parishioners and readers and perhaps Catherine herself — looking for the key to Catherine Lloyd. But the key is hard to find, like the 'secret spring' which secures Catherine's cedar drawer inside which are concealed the watch and ring and those letters which are themselves signs of an absence, 'Long Proofs' (reliable signs? Draft versions?) 'of Love'. It is no wonder that a key is such a common metaphor for the small but crucial clue which will allow a whole disparate mass of otherwise incomprehensible information to fall into place. But it is nice that there is no mention of keys here, literal or metaphoric. The key is misplaced, and can be found in the story of the Widow Goe:

> She spake and trembling, dropp'd upon her knees,
> Heaven in her Eye and in her Hand her Keys:
> And still the more she found her Life decay,
> With greater force she grasp'd those Signs of Sway:
> Then fell and died! ... In haste her Sons drew near,
> And dropp'd, in haste, the tributary Tear,
> Then from th'adhering Clasp the Keys unbound,
> And Consolation for their Sorrows found.

Crabbe is interested in the connection between keys as instruments which enable people to lock or unlock doors (or drawers) and keys as signs, 'Signs of Sway'. The latter, the figurative function of keys, may take two forms. It may take the form of a figure *of speech*, as when we speak of 'the key' to a problem. Or it may take the form of using actual keys in ritual contexts which give them symbolic significance. Keys are often a key element in rites of passage: people are given keys when they come of age, to mark the transition from child to adult; St. Peter has keys which enable him to admit people to Heaven or refuse them admittance and which signify his ability to do so. Keys control the passage across the threshold. The uncertainty about Catherine Lloyd could be said to be about whether such a key exists and whether, if it does, it will be used to admit or exclude. The mention of actual keys in the story of the Widow Goe is powerful in two particular respects. In the first place the material keys become symbolic for her, become 'Signs of Sway', precisely to the extent that they lose their utilitarian function as actual instruments of sway. She can no longer use them. Losing this utilitarian function their signifying power is simultaneously increased and undermined since they are no longer signs of anything; or rather, like Catherine Lloyd's objects, they are signs of the absence of what they are supposed to signify (her sway). The Widow confuses the keys themselves with the ability of human

beings in society to use them and give them symbolic significance; so she clasps powerful symbols of her own impotence,
symbols which are nevertheless, for others, for the living who
have a legal right and physical ability to use them, instruments
and signs working smoothly together to ensure sway.

The image of the keys is powerful in a second respect; or
rather the image of her dead hand clasping the keys. Crabbe
brings to life here the dead metaphor of 'the dead hand of the
past', the hand that continues to exert its sway after it is dead.
This is an image of no-man's-time, a momentary space in which
the keys are held neither by one living generation nor by the
next.

The difficulty which the Widow experiences in passing
through the rite of passage to which St. Peter holds the key
is complemented by her inability to participate properly in the
rites of generational inheritance where the keys to the earthly
kingdom are passed from parent to child. Her unreadiness in
this respect is complemented by the over-readiness of her sons,
who take the keys forcibly from her. Keys, here, are the bour-
geois equivalent of Crowns.

There would be nothing unknown or illegal in Crabbe's mind
or the mind of his contemporary readers, in a widow taking over
the property of her dead husband and the authority in household
and parish which went with it. But the fact that she is, in
conventional fashion, named in terms of her relationship to an
absent person — she is the Widow Goe — emphasizes, perhaps,
a kind of unnaturalness. An extra determination to possess and
command is, implicitly, required of a woman taking what, other
things being equal, would be a man's position. This is a woman
playing a patriarchal role. Her whole life since her husband died
would perhaps — particularly from the sons' point of view — be
a dangerous interregnum in which she is the dead hand of the
father holding sway over the sons.

Chapter 9

The Grimeses

Peter Grimes has been widely recognized as a fine and moving poem, but what makes it moving also makes it troubling. The poem does not fully explain the motives or the meaning of Peter Grimes's conduct, but this partial incomprehension seems right: to explain would, we feel, be to explain away. To an unusual extent the problems which the poem raises seem to be those of life itself rather than of its artistic representation. Perhaps this is why there have been attempts — notably by Benjamin Britten — to rewrite the story. In Britten's opera (the libretto is by Montague Slater) there are, as E.M. Forster pointed out in his 1948 lecture 'George Crabbe and Peter Grimes', 'no ghosts, no father, no murders, no crime on Peter's part except what is caused by the far greater crimes committed against him by society'.[1] Britten has created a liberal-humanist reply to the poem, rather than an operatic version of it. He has tried to

---

[1] *Two Cheers for Democracy* (London, 1951), pp.166–180 (pp.178–9).

explain the story and he has, I believe, explained it away. But in my experience even the most careful readers, talking about the poem, end up producing scenarios for a very different story from the one Crabbe wrote. Indeed, Crabbe seems to invite this in his comments on the poem in the Preface to *The Borough*:

> The character of *Grimes*, his obduracy and apparent want of feeling, his gloomy kind of misanthropy, the progress of his madness, and the horrors of his imagination, I must leave to the judgment and observation of my readers.
>
> (*CPW*, i.354–5)

Crabbe talks as if Grimes had a real life outside the poem (perhaps Crabbe believes he did) and as if the poet were not in control of the meaning of his poem. Forster does the same, only his emphasis is on the possible ambivalences in Crabbe's own life and psyche:

> The interpretations of Freud miss the values of art as infallibly as do those of Marx. They cannot explain values to us, they cannot show us why a work of art is good or how it became good. But they have their subsidiary use: they can indicate the condition of the artist's mind when he was creating, and it is clear that while he was writing 'Peter Grimes' Crabbe was obsessed by the notion of two generations of males being unkind to one another. It is the grandsire-grandson alliance against the tortured adult. The other motive — also to be stressed cautiously — is the attraction-repulsion one. Peter tries to escape from certain places on the stream, but he cannot, he is always drifting back to them. Crabbe is always drifting back in

the spirit to Aldeborough. The poet and his creation share the same inner tension, the same desire for what repels them. Such parallels can often
be found between the experience of a writer, and
the experience of a character in his books, but the
parallel must be drawn lightly by the critic, for the
experiences have usually been transformed out of
all recognition and the moral climate changed.[2]

Forster is right to be hesitant about explanations of a text in
terms of the writer's life or mind, and of deductions about the
latter from the former. He is right too in feeling that the poem
does bring Freudian, and perhaps Marxist themes to mind, but
such explanations are not necessarily *ad hominem* in the way
Forster suggests. The poem is likely to bring Freudian themes
to the mind of a reader who knows nothing about Crabbe's non-
writing life; and not only because it deals with the kind of psychological matters to which Forster refers, but also because (apparently by a coincidence) it seems to be constructed in a way
that recalls the processes of neurosis and psychoanalysis. He is
right to say that, in a poem, 'the experiences have usually been
transformed out of recognition and the moral climate changed';
but that remark seems so peculiarly apposite only because the
poem itself, in its ordering of evidence and of events, recalls those
processes of 'transformation' and 'change' characteristic of the
work of the unconscious in dreams or neuroses and the work of
psychoanalysis. The very title of the poem 'condenses' father
and son in a kind of pun so that the son has no name but the
name of the father. The Peter Grimeses are driven apart by
being forced to live under the same linguistic roof.

One reason why Forster would have been hesitant about
introducing Freudian themes is that they would involve homosexual desire, and in 1949 Forster was probably not prepared to

---

[2] *Two Cheers for Democracy*, pp.176-7.

discuss that publicly. Moreover, to put any sort of sexual construction on the poem seems to impose an *a priori* theory on
a reluctant text. If you try to find sexual implications in the
poem you are left staring at determinedly opaque abstractions.
Just what activities, for instance, are supposed to be included
in 'The grossest Insult and the foulest Wrong' (131) to which
the third apprentice is forced to submit? And while Britten may
have been responding, among other things, to sexual possibilities
in the poem, he makes them little more explicit than Crabbe.
Such interpretations, like the humanist ones Britten does produce, may be products of a modern consciousness. But while
they are hard to read into the poem, they are surely equally
hard to banish from our own minds. We can hardly help, for
instance, being suspicious of the father's unblemished goodness,
and yet there seems to be no warrant for thinking it anything
other than the love it claims to be. Young Peter's behaviour is
announced early on as a fact of character — 'the stubborn boy'
(8) — and his whole subsequent conduct is therefore his own
responsibility. By the same token it is also something like his
fate. Indeed part of what is so troubling about the poem is that
conflation of free-will and determinism, so that Peter's conduct
is a kind of guilty fatality.

Crabbe put a number of short passages from Shakespeare
in front of the poem, as he did later with all the poems in the
1812 *Tales*. These passages encourage us to read the ensuing
poem in terms of its correspondence with, and divergences from,
Shakespearian tragic patterns. Now one thing which *Macbeth*
and *Peter Grimes* have in common is that they are both guilty
of evil courses of action which it is nevertheless their fate to
pursue. But once we have noticed that similarity the difference
stands out clearly: there are no witches in 'Peter Grimes'. The
witches don't solve or abolish the problem of freedom and fate
in *Macbeth*. But they 'embody' that paradox, as elements in a
composite pagan-Christian mythology which is designed to com-

prehend such paradoxes in stories that distinguish and relate this world and another world. The absence of witches from 'Peter Grimes' is therefore the complement of the uncertain status of Peter's visions; an uncertainty greater by one degree than the uncertainty attending the ghosts seen by Macbeth and Hamlet or the 'souls' that visited Richard III.

The father's attempt to inculcate Christian piety and social resignation in his son is important because it is just that kind of thing which might be interposed between the extremes of free-will and determinism which, as things stand, converge to destroy Peter Grimes. Not that the poem is, in any simple way, 'for' established society and 'against' Peter. Our sympathy for Peter clearly increases as he becomes the victim rather than the inflictor of suffering and death. And Crabbe does not see established society as blameless. Certainly Peter Grimes Senior is offered as a wholly positive presence, in his acceptance of humble work, inherited social position, and the traditional responsibilities of a Christian father. Furthermore the borough-burgher who narrates the poem (seldom seen in an ironic light in any of the poems that make up *The Borough*) frequently speaks in the first-person-plural, as if he is uncritically representative of his community. But certain features of established society are criticized, either explicitly (the 'workhouse-clearing men') or implicitly as in the tendency of the local people to look the other way: 'and some, on hearing Cries,/ Said calmly, "*Grimes* is at his Exercise"' (77–8).

Crabbe sees Grimes as a unique figure, uniquely evil and particularly difficult to understand. But Crabbe also wants to see him as a member of human society, an exemplary figure in two senses of the word: an instance of certain general laws of human feeling and an object-lesson to us all. That Grimes is distasteful because of the way in which he subverts the distinction between the inside and the outside (of the body and the body politic) is after all suggested by his name understood as a common noun. The *Concise Oxford Dictionary* defines 'grime' as 'soot or dirt ingrained in some surface, especially the skin'; and as a verb 'grimes' means 'befowls'.

Society itself is notably tardy in punishing Grimes and has its own moral weaknesses; nevertheless, the very extremity of Grimes's behaviour means that, by contrast, society appears relatively blameless. Since Grimes suffers because he rejects normal social standards, society can appear as the 'norm' in that double sense which, by conflating what people do with what people ought to do, can speak of what 'is done' and what is 'not done'. Correlatively Grimes is a 'deviant', a modern word which conflates the unusual and the wrong. Crabbe's fascination with deviants, with marginal figures, which does indeed disrupt the concept of normality, is nevertheless part of an attempt to sustain that concept.

The remarks in Crabbe's Preface on the poems (of which 'Peter Grimes' is one) grouped as 'The Poor of the Borough' are illuminating in this respect:

> The Poor are here almost of necessity introduced,
> for they must be considered, in every place, as a
> large and interesting portion of its inhabitants. I
> am aware of the great difficulty of acquiring just
> notions on the maintenance and management of
> this class of our fellow-subjects.   (*CPW*, i.353)

To 'acquire just notions' means to get a balanced and reliable picture of what in fact goes on, but it also means to decide what ought to be going on. And it is the fact that Crabbe acknowledges the difficulty of finding an 'answer' to the problem of 'maintenance and management' which enables him to go on asking the 'question' as if it were unambiguous. An assumption that 'what is' and 'what ought to be' are in principle the same allows him to concentrate on a restricted range of local evidence which reveals a peculiarly extensive disparity between the two.

The distinction between different kinds of Borough is important in this context. 'Peter Grimes' is part of the long poem *The Borough* in which a burgher from a coastal borough describes his native place in a series of Letters to a friend in an inland borough. 'Peter Grimes' is Letter XXII, the fourth of the sequence dealing with 'The Poor of the Borough'. This format gives rise to the kind of problems of categorization and typicality which we have encountered in *The Village* and 'The Parish Register'. Briefly, it is never clear whether this particular coastal borough is being presented as an instance of the species 'coastal borough' *vis-à-vis* the species 'inland borough' or as a deviant borough in relation to the generic borough represented by the inland borough. And within each letter there is some uncertainty as to whether the examples (for instance, Peter Grimes) are typical or untypical examples of the categories (for instance, The Poor) to which they belong.

It may be objected that neither Crabbe nor his neo-classical predecessors are as dependent on established social norms as a standard of value as this argument would suggest. And in this poem, as elsewhere, Crabbe is indeed committed both to a secular morality and to a morality based on spiritual realities rather than social norms. Peter Grimes suffers because, despite his callousness, he has a 'soul' and a 'conscience'. And insofar as an other-worldly source of values does exist in the poem the conduct of normal society (whether coastal or inland) can be radically criticized without thereby modifying Grimes's peculiar wickedness or his responsibility for his own conduct. But one powerful indication of the poem's doubts about the presence of spiritual, other-worldly forces in this world is the uncertain status of his visions. And it is in this context that 'conscience' becomes crucially important, since it can be interpreted as an internalization either of social norms or of spiritual realities.

Crabbe sharply censures the 'workhouse-clearing men' and their practice of apprenticing orphans from London workhouses

in rural parishes. As he points out, the system was tailor-made
to produce cruelty and neglect since — with the labour it sup-
plied and the initial bounty — it was most attractive to precisely those employers who could least afford to look after the
children properly. However, by picking on this practice Crabbe
draws attention away from similar but less dramatic forms of
cruelty endemic in provincial as well as metropolitan life. The
apprenticing of orphans into other parishes was part of a pervasive attempt to exclude the propertyless from a Settlement in
the 'home' parish. Indeed the operation of the Settlement system might help to explain the Borough's lack of active concern
for Grimes's apprentices and its slowness in bringing Grimes to
book.

It might be expected that, having picked on an extreme
social evil and thus let society in general off the hook, Crabbe
would feel able to acknowledge the workhouse-clearing system
itself as a contributory factor in Grimes's conduct. In fact, the
effect is to emphasize the absolute distinction between such external enabling factors and the interior sources of Grimes's conduct. Crabbe says of Grimes's treatment of the first apprentice:
'He'd now the power he ever loved to show,/ A feeling Being
subject to his Blow' (87–8). The abstract language in which
Grimes's impulse is described is on a different level of explanation from that which details the social factors which enable
him to act upon it so easily. The abstraction marks it also
as an obsessive impulse, which will never find enough victims
to exhaust itself. Consequently it makes sense to call Grimes's
conduct by the name of Crabbe's French contemporary, sadistic.

Nevertheless Crabbe encounters difficulty in reconciling the
two beliefs which are equally important to him: that Grimes is
very different from most people and that he is a member of the
human race. Such difficulties are notably betrayed by his use of
tenses and definite articles:

> He nurst the Feelings these dull Scenes produce,
> And lov'd to stop beside the opening Sluice;
> Where the small Stream, confin'd in narrow bound,
> Ran with a dull, unvaried, sad'ning sound;
> Where all presented to the Eye or Ear,
> Oppress'd the Soul! with Misery, Grief, and Fear.
>
> (199–204)

Peter is clearly involved in delusion, or at least (as we later learn from him) he sees and feels things others do not see and feel. Yet he goes to a place which does itself, we are told, 'produce' such feelings. This is consistent however: going to a place that, almost by convention, does produce such feelings is an aspect of his 'nursing' those feelings. The generalizing definite articles ('the Eye or Ear', 'the Soul') match the generalizing present tense ('produce'): these are things which, in such circumstances, *one feels*. But the last line of the passage pushes the coincidence — between Grimes's particular feelings and the necessary effect on one of that kind of place — a crucial stage further. This would not have been so, paradoxically, if Crabbe had kept to the generalizing present tense and written 'Oppress the Soul'. As it is, the past tense of 'Oppress'd the Soul' emphasizes the particularity of the experience — that it was *his* soul that was oppressed on a particular series of occasions — while the definite article — 'the Soul' — universalizes it. We are with Grimes, indeed we *are* Grimes, just at that moment where he is most irreducibly isolated and singular. The exception is the rule. We are all marginal figures, at the boundaries of normal human existence. Border land is the only kind of land there is. The poem is divided against itself; and this must be related to the self-division it talks *about*, of a man who murders boys like the boy he was when he struck his own father.

Another powerful instance of this complex situation is the

description of how necessity increasingly comes to dominate Peter as he gains his freedom:

> Now liv'd the Youth in freedom, but debarr'd
> From constant Pleasure, and he thought it hard;
> Hard that he could not every Wish obey,
> But must awhile relinquish Ale and Play;
> Hard! that he could not to his Cards attend,
> But must acquire the Money he would spend.
>
> With greedy eye he look'd on all he saw,
> He knew not Justice, and he laugh'd at Law;
> On all he mark'd, he stretch'd his ready Hand;
> He fish'd by Water and he filch'd by Land:
> Oft in the Night has *Peter* dropt his Oar,
> Fled from his Boat and sought for Prey on shore;
> Oft up the Hedge-row glided, on his Back
> Bearing the Orchard's Produce in a Sack,
> Or Farm-yard Load, tugg'd fiercely from the Stack;
> And as these Wrongs to greater numbers rose,
> The more he look'd on all Men as his Foes.
>
> (34–50)

'Oft' Peter and the lines of verse go backwards and forwards. It is the fact that similar acts are repeated over and over again which makes possible the use of a generalizing 'poetic diction', in phrases such as 'Orchard's Produce', 'Farm-yard Load' and the generic definite articles and perhaps the initial capital letters in 'the Hedge-row' and 'the Stack'. These formulae suggest both a clearly ordered world (a world in which each element is clearly an embodiment of the category to which it belongs) and a world of obsessive repetition. A single trip, the description of a single trip or of various different trips, could only collect apples or potatoes or grain. And if Peter only collected apples and potatoes and grain two implications would be lost. We would lose the sense (emphasized by such words as 'fiercely') that Peter's motives are not simply material, but involve an obsessive attempt to re-appropriate a stolen world and punish the world for stealing it. And we would lose the sense that, for the community also, what Peter is stealing is not just things to eat but the social and natural order.

The world he is against confirms in its language what is nevertheless seen as the projection onto it of his own feelings. 'The Orchard's Produce' is a much heavier weight to bear than apples would have been, a weight which becomes explicit in the final couplet:

> And as these Wrongs to greater numbers rose,
> The more he look'd on all Men as his Foes.

In a way these lines are straightforward, since they seem to say something too obvious to mention. But then the fact that it is mentioned suggests that the relation of cause to effect in Peter's life is a strange one. The couplet contains both 'the more he stole the more he hated everyone'. and 'the more he stole the more he thought everyone hated him'. There is of course a natural reciprocity about being a foe, but the implication that something unusual is going on makes us feel the ambivalence of the word 'Foes'. Peter's situation is evoked so effectively because the poem is implicated in the ambivalence it describes.

From a slightly different point of view the problem is one of frequency, of 'how many?' and 'how often?'. The peculiarity of the coastal terrain, the repetition of similar events time after time: these introduce a pervasive uncertainty into the generalizing, generic, definite articles. Did Peter always follow the same route, so that 'the Hedge-row' and 'the Orchard' are one hedgerow and one orchard? Does the fact that Peter 'dropt his Oar' mean that he was sculling? When, in a later passage, Peter turns to 'the blighted Tree' (174) is that one tree or possibly numerous examples of one *kind* of tree? Father and son share

one name, and many of the same events are told twice, once by
the narrator and once by Grimes: so how many boys are there
and how many Peter Grimeses? Peter says he is persecuted by
a father with a 'Boy in either hand' (309); where is the third
apprentice?

'The character of *Grimes*', Crabbe wrote,

> his obduracy and apparent want of feeling, his
> gloomy kind of misanthropy, the progress of his
> madness, and the horrors of his imagination, I
> must leave to the judgment and observation of
> my readers. The mind here exhibited, is one un-
> touched by pity, unstung by remorse, and uncor-
> rected by shame: yet is this hardihood of tem-
> per and spirit broken by want, disease, solitude
> and disappointment, and he becomes the victim
> of a distempered and horror-stricken fancy. It is
> evident, therefore, that no feeble vision, no half-
> visible ghost, not the momentary glance of an un-
> bodied being, nor the half-audible voice of an invis-
> ible one, would be created by the continual work-
> ings of distress on a mind so depraved and flinty.
> The ruffian of *Mr. Scott* has a mind of this nature:
> he has no shame or remorse: but the corrosion of
> hopeless want, the wasting of unabating disease,
> and the gloom of unvaried solitude, will have their
> effect on every nature; and the harder that nature
> is, and the longer time required to work upon it,
> so much the more strong and indelible is the im-
> pression. This is all the reason I am able to give,
> why a man of feeling so dull should yet become in-
> sane, and why the visions of his distempered brain
> should be of so horrible a nature.

> (*CPW*, i.pp.354–5)

This is surely courageous; but what makes it courageous makes it also illusive. The answer to the question posed at the start seems to be arrived at by a slight alteration of its terms and the reversal of its interrogative form. 'How could A become not-A?' Crabbe asks; and answers, 'Because As become not-As'. Two kinds of logic and two conceptions of narrative, intersect here. Such phrases as 'no feeble vision *would be* created', 'the corrosion of hopeless want ... *will have* their effect on every nature; and the harder that nature *is* ... *so much the more* strong and indelible *is* the impression', make the poem exemplify a general law of human feeling and conduct. But the final sentence in effect repeats interrogatively the paradoxical polarity which has just been offered as its explanation, so that the poem becomes an experiment from which a hypothesis is being drawn rather than the exemplification of a prior law.

A slight shift in the terms of the polarity on each occasion is of course necessary to the maintenance of this structure: it means that the answer is always the answer to a slightly different question, the final question not openly undermining the answer which precedes it. This circling back over ground which overlaps, but is never quite coincident with, ground already covered, is precisely what characterizes the conduct of Peter Grimes. The passage from the Preface is thus as much a continuation as an explanation of the poem to which it refers, and both can be described in the same way that Merleau-Ponty, in 'From Mauss to Levi-Strauss', describes Freud's concept of neurosis and Levi-Strauss's concept of myth: 'a spiral thinking which is always trying to hide its fundamental contradiction from itself'.[3] Yet, like neurosis and myth, it reveals as well as conceals contradiction. And what is courageous about the passage (and the poem)

---

[3] *Signs*, translated by R.C. McCleary (Evanston, Illinois, 1964), pp.114–25 (p.121).

is the extent to which it has the courage of its own contradictions: Grimes's delusions are in a sense real ('no feeble vision, no half-visible ghost, nor the momentary glance of an unbodied being') but he is also deluded ('a distempered and horror-stricken fancy ... insane'). The general law of feeling which Crabbe so ambivalently proposes — of a necessary affinity of extreme hardness and extreme vulnerability — is the kind of ambivalence described in post-Freudian theory as 'psychological rigidity'. So that from a psychoanalytical point of view the scarcely controlled movement by which Crabbe turns the single bizarre life into the exemplar of a general law of feeling is as impressive as it is confused.

The ambivalence of Crabbe's discussion of 'the character of *Grimes*' affects, among other things, the meaning of the word 'character'. Crabbe is trying to use the word in that unitary sense which implies a narrative idea of life. Yet there is clearly a possibility that Grimes's is a life that cannot be characterized, that he is a man whose Life cannot be constructed. Crabbe's statement asserts and denies the availability of this Life, and therefore the structural identity of a life and a Life.

Of course the poem itself does not even pretend to know 'the whole story'. Its narrator is quite openly piecing together his narrative from what evidence is available: court hearings, what locals and tourists have witnessed, what Peter himself eventually says, and so on. And there is no pretence that the story is being told in chronological order. But these features do not in themselves indicate the depth of the poem's uncertainty about the true pattern of cause and effect in Peter's existence. Something of this uncertainty has already been suggested. We can take a further step by attending more carefully than we have done so far to the relationship between the order and frequency of events as they occur in the text and the implied actual order and frequency of events.[4]

---

[4]   The treatment of this relationship in modern narrative theory is

In the first thirty-three lines of the poem, where Peter's early life and his father's death are described, we hear about some of the events retrospectively, through Peter's drunken recollection of them. Officially this reordering of events is not supposed to alter their significance, the sequence of cause and effect read into them. But the tenses suggest uncertainty both about the frequency with which and the order in which events took place. The poem begins by describing a state of affairs in the past:

> Old *Peter Grimes* made Fishing his employ,
> His Wife he cabin'd with him and his Boy,
> And seem'd that Life laborious to enjoy:
> To Town came quiet *Peter* with his Fish,
> And had of all a civil word and wish.
> He left his Trade upon the Sabbath-Day,
> And took young *Peter* in his hand to pray;
>
> (1–7)

This describes repeated actions which constitute a state of affairs, rather than unique events. 'He left his Trade upon the Sabbath-Day' means 'he used to leave his trade' on Sundays, not that one Sunday he decided to give up his job and devote his life to religious education. But it is characteristic of English — as we have seen in 'The Parish Register' — that these two kinds of pastness use the same verbal form. And it is because they do so that an uncertainty as to whether we are dealing with a single or a recurrent event can appear in the lines that follow:

> But soon the stubborn Boy from care broke loose,
> At first refus'd, then added his abuse:
> His Father's Love he scorn'd, his Power defied,
> But being drunk, wept sorely when he died.
>
> (8–11)

---

usefully discussed in J. Culler, *The Pursuit of Signs: semiotics, literature, deconstruction* (London, 1981), pp.169–187.

Was the boy always stubborn or is this a new development? And
while common sense tells us that the father's death is a unique
event, which breaks up the state of affairs established by the
son's rebellion, do not these actual lines — 'His Father's Love he
scorn'd, his Power defied,/ But being drunk, wept sorely when
he died' — suggest that the father died whenever the son got
drunk? Or that it was the son who died and the father who got
drunk? Such fanciful readings are prompted by the awkward way
in which the couplet is put together. Yet that awkwardness, and
the phantom presence of other possible narratives to which it
gives rise, are essential to the powerful effect the lines do have.
They reproduce the shock of death as a traumatic event: an event
so disturbing that it cannot be incorporated into a person's sense
of the continuity of their life and, consequently, seems to repeat
itself covertly in all their subsequent experience.

In the drunkenness which follows as well as precedes his
father's death, Peter remembers events prior to that death:

> How, when the Father in his Bible read,
> He in contempt and anger left the Shed:
> 'It is the Word of Life,' the Parent cried;
> — 'This is the Life itself,' the Boy replied.
>
> (16–19)

The first two lines imply a recurring occasion, the next two a
single occasion: an uncertainty that suggests very powerfully a
harrowing banality in the confrontations of father and son but
of course also makes it impossible to tell what 'really' happened.
And then, buried deeper in parenthesis, the son remembers how
the father, cursing him, had himself recalled an event even further back in the past:

> The Father groan'd — 'If thou are old,' said he,
> 'And hast a Son — thou wilt remember me:
> Thy Mother left me in an Happy Time,

Thou kill'dst not her — Heav'n spares the double Crime.'
    On an Inn-settle, in his maudlin Grief,
    This he revolv'd and drank for his Relief.
                                                    (28–33)

Now if it is so important to the poem that Peter's impulses
and conduct are essentially uncaused (are his responsibility and
his fate) it is surely significant that this earlier event should be
moved out of its chronological position, to be acknowledged in
a parenthetical retrospect. It suggests that it is proper to ask
'Soon after what did the stubborn boy break loose?' and even
'Soon after what did the boy become stubborn?'

Furthermore the dialogue between father and son can itself
be re-interpreted so as to make more sense of the son's subsequent conduct. The father puts the son in a kind of double-bind.
In effect he accuses the son of the desire to kill the mother, but
does so in a way that makes it difficult for the son to realize
that this is what the father is doing, and so makes it difficult
for him to reject the accusation: the father is, on the face of it,
absolving him from actual guilt, and the mother is already dead.
By doing this as he warns his son how the son will feel when
he in his turn becomes a father, Grimes Senior utters a curse
disguised as a warning. He puts his son in the way of inflicting
his anger and unwitting guilt on boys like himself. The father
implants a guilty motive by absolving him from a guilty act, and
ensures that there is no action the son can take to get rid of the
guilt: all he can do is come to deserve it. In this way what might
have been a mitigating factor (the mother's death) is made to
exacerbate his guilt. An emotional formation of this kind surely
asserts itself when the court acquits Peter with the words:

'Keep fast your Hatchway when you've Boys who climb.'
    This hit the Conscience, and he colour'd more
    Than for the closest questions put before.
                                                    (115–17)

But an analysis of this kind does raise problems. We can 'expose' what the father says and relate it to the son's subsequent actions and to the prior death of the mother; we can uncover the mechanisms of concealment in these passages in an attempt to construct an alternative narrative. But just who and what are we thereby exposing: Peter Grimes's life and psyche or George Crabbe's life and psyche? (In Freud's discussion of *Hamlet* it is similarly unclear whether he is talking about Hamlet's psyche or Shakespeare's.) Moreover in constructing an alternating narrative out of and against the official one I may only have reversed the latter's moralism, shifting the 'blame' from the son's evil nature to the false-love of the father.

The mistake however is to look for a simple true narrative. The poem's ability to evoke so powerfully the relationship between father and son, to reveal the processes by which the father's 'love' helps to produce the son's 'evil', certainly depends upon its (the poem's) co-operation with the father in doing so. But this does not mean that what the poem really tells us is that the blame really lies with the father and the society. Instead, within the official view, and as its hidden condition, is the possibility of the contrary view.

Kinds of psychoanalytic thinking which see language playing a constitutive rather than a merely representational role in the construction of human reality are relevant to my argument here. Merleau-Ponty's analysis of tense-acquisition in relation to psychological rigidity and jealousy seems particularly pertinent:

> It is in the phase of the surpassing of jealousy that one notices the appearance of a link between the affective phenomenon and the linguistic phenomenon: jealousy is overcome thanks to the construction of a scheme of past-present-future. In effect jealousy in this subject consists in a rigid attachment to his present — that is to the situation

of the 'latest-born' which was hitherto his own. He considered the present to be absolute. Now, on the contrary, we can say that from the moment when he consents to be no longer the latest born, to become in relation to the new baby what his eldest brother had until then been in relation to him, he replaces his attitude of 'my place has been taken' with another whose scheme might be 'I *have been* the youngest, but I *am* the youngest no longer, and I *will become* the biggest'.[5]

This does seem relevant to 'Peter Grimes' where alterations in the child's position in the family (death of mother, death of father) appear in the context of a grammatical inability to deal with past events which changed one state of affairs into another state of affairs.

But of course I have identified similar difficulties with time and tense in other poems, including *The Village* where questions of family, gender and sexual desire do not seem to be so much in evidence. Furthermore these difficulties appear to have an historical significance which psychoanalytic explanations of whatever kind tend to obscure. The child in Merleau-Ponty's description gives up 'a rigid attachment to his present' by substituting one kind of 'I am' (a kind which is defined by its difference from 'I was' and 'I shall be') for another kind of 'I am' (defined by its difference from 'I am not'). And in Crabbe's work it is frequently hard to know which kind of present tense we are dealing with. But this confusion is also explicable in terms of Crabbe's uncertain relationship to an historically specific narrative idea of life which itself offers the universalising present (Merleau-Ponty's 'absolute' present) as the tense to which all other tenses can be happily subordinated.

---

[5] *The Primacy of Perception*, translated by W. Cobb and others (Evanston, Illinois, 1964), p.110.

Psychoanalytic explanations must also contend with the historical perspectives which Crabbe himself seems to encourage by putting passages from Shakespeare at the beginning of his poem. That juxtaposition encourages us to think about alterations in the relation between secular and supernatural realities and between different levels of secular authority. If society, nature and supernatural realities all seem to speak to Peter Grimes in his father's voice this seems to require an explanation that the poem does not offer but which psychoanalysis is eager to provide. But the likeness between fathers, Kings and God are written *openly* into the language of the plays to which Crabbe alludes.

Perhaps however the difference between Shakespeare and Crabbe in this respect though real is not so vast as it may initially appear. Certainly Peter Grimes Senior is not a divinely appointed monarch — he doesn't even rule over a quasi-feudal household like the Earl's in 'Delay has Danger' — but his relationship to his son is of a patriarchal kind. He is his son's master as well as father, the head of a working household. Furthermore the son's violence against his father is described as a 'sacrilegious Blow' as if the father is indeed one of God's substitutes. And if Peter Grimes Junior is his father's quasi-apprentice as well as his son, the orphaned apprentices are Peter's own quasi-children: he stands to them *in loco parentis*. Father and son share the one name. It is as if there is an insufficient number of proper names to go round so that the two men are reduced to being identical members of a single category. The poem's ostensible differentiation between individuals, as well as its ostensible sequence of cause and effect, is unstable. Cause and effect seem reversible, difference and similarity confused.

These things make more sense if they are seen as part of a patriarchal ordering which is both powerful and illusive. How small or how great is the difference between a father who is a kind of master and a master who is a kind of father? Even Peter's sadistic treatment of his apprentices makes more sense if we see in it a terrible example of the patriarchal combination of economic or political relationship with kin or sexual relationship.

Poems like 'Delay has Danger' and 'The Patron' are untypical of Crabbe's tales in describing the explicitly patriarchal regime of a noble household. But they also call that ordering of reality into question. In most of Crabbe's tales, as in 'Peter Grimes', patriarchal order initially seems to be less evident or less plausible, but is in fact a very powerful presence. These stories about professional people, farmers and tradespeople are all in their way stories about households and patronage. They are stories about masters and mistresses in relation to apprentices, servants, shopmen, wards and dependent 'friends'. And if masters or apprentices or wards seem to project unresolved familial conflicts onto one another such overlaps are particularly troubling for Crabbe because in a sense there is nothing odd about them at all. A patron *is* a paternal figure, a master *does* stand *in loco parentis*.

Chapter 10

The Life of Allen Booth

I have called this chapter 'The Life of Allen Booth' so as to involve readers in advance in the problems I am going to discuss. My argument hinges on whether or not there is an ambiguity in my title, and if there is whether it's a significant one. The ambiguity is that 'Life' could either refer to the existence of Allen Booth or to the story of the existence of Allen Booth. A leitmotif of my argument in this book has been that during the eighteenth century and well into the period of Crabbe's writing life the conflation of those two meanings was usual, insistent, and deliberate. Some remarks of Samuel Johnson in *The Rambler*, 41 for 7 August 1750 will effectively recapitulate the argument. 'Memory', writes Johnson,

> is the purveyor of reason, the power which places those images before the mind upon which the judgement is to be exercised, and which treasures up the determinations that are once passed, as the rules of future action, or grounds of subsequent

conclusions.

It is, indeed, the faculty of remembrance, which may be said to place us in the class of moral agents. If we were to act only in consequence of some immediate impulse, and receive no direction from internal motives of choice, we should be pushed forward by an invincible fatality, without power or reason for the most part to prefer one thing to another, because we could make no comparison but of objects which might both happen to be present.[1]

The implication of this passage is, as Martin Golding puts it, that 'the subject reviews his previous actions and determines his continuing life by reference to maxims and insights derived as it were from set pieces in his memory. Our capacity, that is, to conduct ourselves morally, depends in fact on our capacity to see our lives as a narrative'.

It is this 'narrative idea of the moral life', this insistence that to see one's life for what it really is means seeing it as a Life, which 'The Parting Hour' involves and is fundamentally about. My argument is that the poem is haunted by the possibility that there is no such thing as a Life, no connection between existence and biography, but is also committed to the assumption that there is. The poem tries to entertain the distinction between existence and biography in a way that will appear to reaffirm that no such distinction exists. The poem is a device for attempting to represent incompatible beliefs as if they are compatible. It is a simultaneous acknowledgement and evasion of incompatible beliefs. The mechanisms in it are mechanisms for having your cake and eating it, for not letting your left hand know what your

---

[1] *The Works of Samuel Johnson*, Volume III, *The Rambler*, edited by W.J. Bate and A.B. Strauss (New Haven, Connecticut, 1969), p.223.

right hand is doing. It will be evident from these various formulations that I'm suggesting, once again, that Crabbe's poetry has a structure which is very similar to the structure which Freud attributes to neurosis and which Levi-Strauss attributes to myth. I shall return to the significance of these analogies later. What I shall try to do first of all is prove my contention about the structure and function of the poem itself.

The poem begins with two paragraphs whose argument the ensuing poem is in some way, we take it, going to exemplify:

> Minutely trace man's life; year after year,
> Through all his days let all his deeds appear,
> And then, though some may in that life be strange,
> Yet there appears no vast nor sudden change:
> The links that bind those various deeds are seen,
> And no mysterious void is left between.
>
> But let these binding links be all destroy'd,
> All that through years he suffer'd or enjoy'd;
> Let that vast gap be made, and then behold —
> This was the youth, and he is thus when old;
> Then we at once the work of Time survey,
> And in an instant see a life's decay;
> Plan mixt with pity in our bosoms rise,
> And sorrow takes new sadness from surprise.
>
> (1–14)

The first paragraph is clearly using the word 'Life' in the unitary sense I have been describing. There is no temptation to ask whether the poem is referring to a kind of existence or a kind of biography. The word 'trace' in the first line is a key word in this context. It means to follow, search out; but also to copy, as with tracing paper. If you imagine a perfectly transparent piece of tracing paper placed over a line drawing which is then traced on the paper, the tracing does not independently appear: the distinction between the tracing and the traced does not exist.

But what about the second paragraph? This is trickier. It does make the distinction between existence and biography, but it does so covertly. Because while it can't refer to *both*, it can refer to *either*. That it to say, it is not definitely about a kind of biography rather than a kind of existence; and it is not definitely about a kind of existence rather than a kind of biography. It could be referring to either a special kind of existence — an existence (one's own or another's) which has been in some way broken in two — or to a kind of biography, a particular way of writing the biography of anybody. What it can't do is refer to both since if it refers to a kind of existence it is precisely to a *special* kind of existence, that kind whose full Life, as described in paragraph one, cannot be written. So this second paragraph subverts the concept of a Life, but it does so covertly.

But how is it that the ensuing story can illustrate paragraph two in its various possible meanings, not to say paragraph one as well, without clearly bringing out the contradictions which are so far only latent? In the rest of this chapter I shall attempt to show how this is done.

The second paragraph of the poem describes a diptych: 'This was the youth, and he is thus when old'. In the actual story which follows we are indeed presented with such a diptych, but in reversed order: the Age of Allen and Judith is followed by their Youth:

> Beneath yon tree, observe an ancient Pair —
> A sleeping man; a woman in her chair, ...
> To *David Booth*, his fourth and last-born boy,
> *Allen* his name, was more than common joy; ...
> His early love he fix'd upon a fair
> And gentle Maid — they were a handsome pair.
> (15–16, 32–3, 40–1)

By reversing the order of Youth and Age in this way the poem

can in fact combine the illustration of the second paragraph with
the illustration of the first. Age is juxtaposed to Youth which is
the start of an unbroken sequence, year after year, link by link
until, so we expect, we come round to Age again. This doesn't
quite happen however: a quite different vast gap appears, the
binding links are all destroyed *again*, with Allen's forty year
absence, this time in such a way as to suggest that the previous
gap between Age and Youth was in the biography rather than in
the existence and that this second gap is in the existence rather
than in the biography. Now if this is the case the illustration of
paragraph one ought to be impossible: Allen Booth would seem
to be an example of an existence whose biography cannot be
written. In which case the concept of a Life disintegrates. But
we *do* get the Life of Allen Booth. Crabbe enables it to exist by
basing the unity of Allen's existence in Allen's memory; or, more
specifically, in his ability to put himself in position as spectator
of his own life conceived as a narrative in the third person.

The forty-year gap is introduced in the following way:

> But when return'd the Youth? — the Youth no more
> Return'd exulting to his native shore;
> But forty years were pass'd, and then there came
> A worn-out man, with wither'd limbs and lame;
> (183–6)

Now it is surely the reader (and in another sense the landbound
observer) who experiences the events in the manner described, as
a juxtaposition, very much in the manner of the poem's second
paragraph:

> This was the youth, and he is thus when old;
> Then we at once the work of Time survey,
> And in an instant see a life's decay;
> Pain mixt with pity in our bosoms rise,
> And sorrow takes new sadness from surprise.

What is remarkable however is that this way of seeing is in fact shared by Allen himself. He too is a spectator of his life:

> He was alone; he press'd the very place
> Of the sad parting, of the last embrace:
> There stood his parents, there retir'd the Maid,
> So fond, so tender, and so much afraid;
> And on that spot, through many a year, his mind
> Turn'd mournful back, half sinking, half resign'd.
>
>   (193–8)

Allen is the spectator of his own life by virtue of his memory, which has, at this point and on previous occasions, 'place(d) those images before the mind' as Johnson put it. Yet there is a price to be paid. For Allen's experience here also corresponds to a more modern, romantic, notion of self-division: as alienation, loss, an experience bordering on schizoid hallucination. Indeed Allen's previous self is so powerfully present to him that the scene may well recall Johnson's description of our condition when we act *without* the 'faculty of remembrance', when we are 'pushed forward by invincible fatality, without power or reason for the most part to prefer one thing to another, because we could make no comparison but of objects which might both happen to be present'.

But whatever else it may be, this description of Allen's departure and return is certainly an instance of juxtaposition in the manner of the poem's second paragraph, rather than of unbroken continuity in the manner of its first paragraph. Yet the gap of forty years *is* eventually closed — by Allen's own story-telling. The poem attempts to make that gap compatible with a narrative idea of life by making the primary problem of Allen's life his faulty memory; the difficulty he has in arranging the events of that period in their proper sequence, which includes the attempt to distinguish between a real experience and a dream or fantasy of it. The poem can give us Allen's Life if Allen can: it is committed to Allen as its only source. Insofar as Allen can tell Judith his Life the tragic gap in his experience is healed in the same process as the gap in his biography is healed; and precisely to the extent that these hiatuses can be healed they cease to be *distinct* hiatuses at all. Existence and biography, whose separation the poem has insistently entertained, slide together again, and the distinction disappears.

I now want to look at a number of sections of the poem very closely so as to show in rather more detail how this process of both entertaining and denying contradiction works. First of all I shall say something about Allen's telling of his story to Judith. Then I shall examine the section of the poem which describes the couple's youth and their separation. And finally I shall look at Allen's description of his experience after he landed back on his native shore.

I said that the contradictions in the poem can be given an apparent resolution insofar as Allen can arrange his life into a sequential narrative. But can he? Officially the answer is that he can. The joins in the forty-year section of his life are formulations of the following kind:

> First he related — How he left the shore,
>
> $\qquad\qquad\qquad\qquad\qquad$ (313)

> He next related how he found a way,
> Guideless and grieving, to Campeachy-Bay:
>
> $\qquad\qquad\qquad\qquad\qquad$ (372-3)

> And then he told how in a calm distress'd,
> Day after day his soul was sick of rest;
>
> $\qquad\qquad\qquad\qquad\qquad$ (396-7)

> He then describ'd the gloom, the dread he found,
> When first he landed on the chosen ground,
>
> $\qquad\qquad\qquad\qquad\qquad$ (426-7)

Now these formulae assert that Allen narrated his story in the order of the actual events of which it tells, in chronological order; and that coincidence is after all the justification for the poem conflating the two and using indirect reported speech. The poem gives us Allen's story-telling, but it gives it to us as a narrative in the third person. Allen himself, its source, can in principle stand in the same relation to his Life as we readers can.

But one of the things this story describes is how he frequently suffered from hallucinations, from thinking he was back in England when in fact he was at sea or thinking he was in South America with his wife and children when in fact he was back in England. He suffered from confusions, that is to say, about the sequence of his existence. And he still suffers from such dreams and hallucinations. There is surely a tension here. For if he's still suffering from them, if he's in the state we see him as being in, it seems rather unlikely that he actually told the story through in the chronological order of the events it describes. And of course an awful lot hangs on that: if he can't do it the poem can't either, since the poem has committed itself to him as the sole source of its knowledge of his existence during those forty years. Of course it may be said that to argue in this way is to take those formulae ('he first related ... And then he told') in an unfairly literal manner. Some work of reconstruction from a number of bits of story-telling may be allowed. We may say that 'First he related' really means 'He related how first'; that 'And then he told' really means 'And he told how then'. Also we could argue that though he still suffers from confusion from time to time, he at other times knows it is confusion: he, and therefore we, can in fact distinguish between what is happening and what he sometimes believes is happening but which in fact happened in the past. Thus the poem seems to end with just such a clarification: "My God! 'twas but a dream".

If we want to pin down the contradictions we have to move in even closer to the poem:

He then describ'd the gloom, the dread he found,
When first he landed on the chosen ground,
Where undefin'd was all he hoped and fear'd,
And how confus'd and troubled all appear'd;
His thoughts in past and present scenes employ'd,
All views in future blighted and destroy'd:
His were a medley of bewild'ring themes,
Sad as realities, and wild as dreams.

Here his relation closes, but his mind
Flies back again some resting-place to find;
(426–35)

Ostensibly this passage describes Allen now looking back, with
clarity, at a period of previous confusion. But this distinction
between a confusion in what is seen and a clarity in the seeing
is also questioned. The crucial lines are

His were a medley of bewild'ring themes,
Sad as realities, and wild as dreams.

To what period of time do these lines refer? I think that first
of all, coming on the lines after reading the previous ones, we in
fact take them to refer to the later period, to his telling. But
the lines which follow change the way in which we read the couplet. In the perspective of these subsequent lines, written in the
present tense, the confusion is in the past and is to do with the
final events which he told us *about.* The ambiguity of the word
'relation' is clearly crucial here: it conflates, like a Life, what is
related and the relating of it. Consequently the word also aims
to bring into coherent relationship Allen as the subject of what
is narrated and Allen as the subject of the act of relation. But in
this context, where two readings of the couplet are possible, the
assertion of that identity is at the price of introducing a covert
incoherence, division, into the concept. Why does this happen?
I think it is because in this poem Crabbe is trying to co-

ordinate distinct temporal trajectories which can't in fact be co-
ordinated. Imagine for a moment that the poem ended with

> His were a medley of bewild'ring themes,
> Sad as realities, and wild as dreams.

If it did so, the whole sequence from Youth to Age could take
place easily in the simple past tense, which can refer to specific
actions and to continuing situations in the past: 'They were in
love when they were young, later they parted, then after forty
years he came back, and he spent the evening of his days trying
to tell her what he'd been doing'. This would be a way of giving
us the Life in the manner of paragraph one, as an unbroken
sequence: a sequence of frames passing before us for review, the
simple past tense functioning happily as a particular mode of the
universal present tense which governs the narrative idea of life.
What happened to Allen Booth is simply a particular instance
of what happens to human beings, of The Life of Man from birth
to death. There is however also an actual present tense in this
poem:

> Beneath yon tree, observe an ancient Pair —
> A sleeping man; a woman, in her chair,
>
> (15–16)

Now this present tense is also compatible with the universal
present tense, since it is the present of an action at a distance,
framed for our view like the pictures in the gallery Johnson
presents to us in 'The Vanity of Human Wishes'. We are being asked to look at a framed scene. And the other half of this
diptych can be in a past tense without disturbing the pictorial,
observational mode, as in 'This was the Youth and he is thus
when old'.

So both these temporal schemes are compatible with the
universal present tense. The trouble comes in the attempt to
combine them. In attempting to combine the exemplification of

paragraphs one and two Crabbe has to bring a past which happens at a distance into a present which happens at a distance. And you can see the join in the passage I discussed. It is at that point particularly, where it has to stitch the two temporal trajectories together that one gets the sense of a wholly different temporal trajectory trying to make itself felt, in which a different kind of past is linked to a different kind of present in a way which does indeed threaten the universal present tense. And this trajectory would go something like: 'They used to be lovers but then he went away; however recently he has returned and he is now telling her his story'. There is in fact a tension right through the poem, from the description of Youth onwards, between different kinds of pastness; but the tension need not make itself so clearly felt because the English past simple tense is very flexible. The phrase 'he went', for instance, can refer to a single event in the past or to a recurrent event. And in the latter case we cannot always tell (as we can with 'he used to go') if this past is being linked to the present in which it is mentioned. In Crabbe's poem, it is as the past has to approach closer and closer to the person who is by now the source of our knowledge of it, in the present of 'Beneath yon tree', and approach it in such a way that there shall seem to be no 'gap', that the problem becomes really acute. It is then that one feels the pressure of a tense, a relationship between a kind of past and a kind of present, which can find no room in the poem. This is the tense, which finds its classic literary manifestation in 'The Prelude', of 'he has gone'.[2] Asserting the continual presence, possession, of what is nevertheless gone, it also refers to the present discourse of the narrator and includes that in the narrative. It suggests that 'he went' really meant 'he used to go'. It also implies the possibility of a presently unformed future. In Crabbe's poem

---

[2] J. and Z. Boyd, 'The Perfect of Experience', *Studies in Romanticism*, 16 (1977), pp.3-13.

this tense is unable to speak its name. And so it is no accident that Allen is preparing to die, has no future, is faced towards the past; otherwise he might have spoken to the poem's non-existent narrator. Pretty well a corpse Allen remains luckily at a distance, in a frame, because the poem has, from the start, 'framed' him. But he does also break out of that frame. When he cries at the end "My God! 'twas but a dream", it is as if he is disappearing towards us into the auditorium like a figure in one of the old '3D' movies.

I suggested that the problems are less acute in the passages describing the couple's early life. But we should be able to find evidence of them:

> To *David Booth*, his fourth and last-born boy,
> *Allen* his name, was more than common joy;
> And as the child grew up, there seem'd in him
> A more than common life in every limb;
> A strong and handsome stripling he became,
> And the gay spirit answer'd to the frame;
> A lighter, happier lad was never seen,
> For ever easy, cheerful, or serene;
> His early love he fix'd upon a fair
> And gentle Maid — they were a handsome pair.
>
> They at an infant-school together play'd,
> Where the foundation of their love was laid;
> The boyish champion would his choice attend
> In every sport, in every fray defend.
> As prospects open'd and as life advanc'd,
> They walk'd together, they together danc'd;
> On all occasions, from their early years,
> They mix'd their joys and sorrows, hopes and fears;
> Each heart was anxious, till it could impart
> Its daily feelings to its kindred heart;
> As years increas'd, unnumber'd petty wars

Broke out between them; jealousies and jars;
Causeless indeed, and follow'd by a peace,
That gave to love — growth, vigour, and increase.
Whilst yet a boy, when other minds are void,
Domestic thoughts young *Allen*'s hours employ'd;
Judith in gaining hearts had no concern,
Rather intent the Matron's part to learn;
Thus early prudent and sedate they grew,
While lovers, thoughtful — and, though children, true.
To either's parents not a day appear'd,
When with this love they might have interfer'd:
Childish at first, they car'd not to restrain;
And strong at last, they saw restriction vain;
Nor knew they when that passion to reprove —
Now idle fondness, now resistless love.

So while the waters rise, the children tread
On the broad *Estuary*'s sandy bed;
But soon the channel fills, from side to side
Comes danger rolling with the deep'ning tide;
Yet none who saw the rapid current flow,
Could the first instant of that danger know.

(32–73)

According to my argument this passage has to be three incompatible things. It has to be the first term of a juxtaposition, in the biography, of Age and Youth. It also has to be the first term of a juxtaposition, in the existence, of Youth and Age. And finally, it has to be the second term of a contrast between juxtaposition and unbroken sequence.

Now these are clearly distinct functions, but are they really incompatible? They *are* incompatible, for the following reason: the very same lines are required to be both one term of a juxtaposition (one frame of a diptych showing Age and Youth) and part of the kind of unbroken sequentiality to which such juxtaposition is being contrasted. The passage is therefore required to be in contrast to itself.

But it doesn't, I think, read as if it is, even after you've worked out that it must be. Why not? My explanation is as follows.

The first two functions of the passage are quite easily reconciled. Youth, as one frame of a diptych, will have the same *form* whether it is the beginning of an existence or the end of a biography.

Secondly, one frame of a diptych can also, strange as this may seem, be not too different in *form* from an unbroken sequence, or part of an unbroken sequence. The first paragraph says that

> Though some may in that life be strange,
> Yet there appears no vast nor sudden change:

The question is 'how vast is vast?', or 'when is a change not a change?' (how many minutes are there in a parting hour?). Nevertheless, since a passage of poetry is in fact sequential and cannot be literally a framed picture or a still-photograph, the difference between a passage of poetry aspiring to the condition of a framed picture and one presenting an unbroken sequence in which change is not very noticeable may be hard to decipher.

It ought to be possible to decipher it however, to spot in the passage I have quoted a tension between the requirement that things should be changing and the requirement that nothing should be changing. It should be possible to decide what sense to give to the simple past tense in which the lines are written. And if we re-read the passage with this problem in mind we should be struck by a curious fact: the story is precisely *about* the problem of working out whether anything is changing or not, about a relationship which seems both not to change and to change dramatically. In other words the poem has brilliantly hidden the logical-structural problem, given it an apparent resolution according to the textbook method for hiding valuables: by putting them right where they stare you in the face. It has hidden the logical-structural problems by decanting them into the human contents of the story, making them the explicit contents of the human situation.

One would be hard put to it to say whether the lines describe a situation or a sequence of events because the human relationship is always the same only more so:

> As years increas'd, unnumber'd petty wars
> Broke out between them; jealousies and jars;
> Causeless indeed, and follow'd by a peace,
> That gave to love — growth, vigour and increase.

Furthermore if we still feel uncertain about what it is that we are witnessing, that uncertainty is itself resolved by being acknowledged in a displaced form, as the uncertainty of the parents in the story:

> To either's parents not a day appear'd,
> When with this love they might have interfer'd:
> Childish at first, they car'd not to restrain;
> And strong at last, they saw restriction vain;
> Nor knew they when that passion to reprove —
> Now idle fondness, now resistless love.

Crabbe has represented a human relationship characterized by just that unbroken sequentiality which can suddenly seem to have, at some indefinable point, changed completely, to have the shape of two juxtaposed stills, a diptych, 'Now idle fondness, now resistless love'.

This does not in fact magic the contradiction away. But it does mean that to track down evidence of it we need to refuse the invitation to become absorbed in the human contents of the story and return to the linguistic surface of the text. For instance what does the word 'while' mean in the line 'While lovers thoughtful —

and, though children, true'? Does it mean 'when' or 'although'?
Were they lovers when they were children? 'Thus early prudent
and sedate they grew' is not really compatible with

> The boyish champion would his choice attend
> In every sport, in every fray defend.

or with

> And the gay spirit answer'd to the frame;
> A lighter, happier lad was never seen,

It seems that in describing a 'slow-sudden' relationship, one
which possesses just that kind of unbroken sequentiality that
can retrospectively be seen as a dramatic alteration the writing
has to submit to a degree of ambivalence which reproduces that
double nature at every moment. The passage is composed of
descriptions which neither clearly describe a single condition nor
clearly describe an unbroken sequence. It is never clear whether
at any one moment we are getting the description of a slightly
different span of time from the same point of view or the same
span of time from a slightly different point of view. It is never
quite clear how we are to interpret this past tense. It could be
objected that this evokes very effectively the kind of relationship to which the parents have to respond in the way they do.
But this does not resolve the problem, because the description
of the parents' response is itself ambivalent in exactly the same
way. Does 'Now idle fondness, now resistless love' mean that
the parents felt that the relationship had by gradual molecular
alteration undergone a total transformation, or that they felt
as if it had continually been 'now one thing and now another'.
And even the extremes referred to are not really very like the
extremes referred to earlier: the childhood affection was never
'idle', and the main characteristic of it as it developed seemed
to be its domesticity, the couple having as it were already become in manner and in feeling the 'sober' and 'prudent' husband

and wife they presumably expect to be in reality later on. And finally, it's worth noting that the word 'resistless' rhymes with 'listless'; and that it can mean 'unresisting' as well as irresistible.

So the passage is indeed ambivalent, despite its attempts to disguise its ambivalence as the difficulty of the human relationship it describes. The passage in fact describes two kinds of development. From one point of view the sexuality of the relationship builds up very gradually so that the strength of its eventual demands seems both inevitable and strange. From another point of view what is described is the gradual avoidance-suppression of sexuality as the relationship develops from a childhood sibling-like one into a thoroughly tamed domesticity.

The simile which concludes the quoted passage, of the tide rising on the unwary children as they 'tread/ On the broad *Estuary*'s sandy bed' curiously emphasizes this ambivalence. What is curious about it is the overlap between tenor and vehicle: Allen and Judith after all *are* children, and *do* live by the sea. This curiously uncertain — even reversible — relationship between the literal and the figurative means that a traditional figure associating sexuality and danger — 'the rising tide of passion' — seems *also* to polarize the two in a way that becomes significant later on.

So far in my discussion I have shown how Crabbe tries to resolve the logical problems of exemplifying the first two paragraphs of the poem by decanting them into the human relationships. He tries and to a considerable extent he succeeds. But, as we have seen, he doesn't altogether succeed. If you check carefully enough you find that tendencies are being attributed to the relationships, patterns of development, which are simply incompatible.

However at this point I want to do something of rather doubtful validity. I want to assume that Allen and Judith really existed and see how far one can reconstruct from the evidence provided a real social context that might indeed explain why

their relationship is described in contradictory ways. Or, to put
it another way, I want to suggest the sort of facts which might
be brought into play by the novel for which this poem could be
the cryptic scenario.

Most of the information we are given about the social circumstances and internal relations of the families of Allen and
Judith comes from the sequence I have already discussed. Allen
is David's Booth's 'fourth and last-born boy'. The youngest
son in a family in rather straitened circumstances, he would,
for reasons of economics and internal family politics, expect a
long engagement. So much is more or less explicit. All we know
about Judith's family is what emphasizes the similarity of social
position, and therefore the likelihood of their being approved of
as childhood friends. And 'In either house were men and maids
unwed,/ Hopes to be sooth'd, and tempers to be led' (76–7).
Allen asks 'Why should our friends be thus dissatisfied?' (89),
and by 'friends' he would mean families. Indeed, early editions
of the poem say that 'To either parents not a day appear'd', as if
uncertain whether Allen and Judith belong to different families;
a locution 'corrected' by Crabbe's modern editors to 'To either's
parents' (62).

At this point we may think we are on to some answers, answers for which our reading of 'The Parish Register' especially
may have prepared us. For instance if both families are on the
same social level and both hard-up the children will most naturally be friends. But just the same reason could make it important for each family, if they are to preserve their social status,
either to insist on a long engagement or to try to marry their children *above* their own station. The relationship between Allen's
mother and Judith suggests this: the mother thinks Judith 'vain'
(84) not because she will take Allen up in the world but because
she will ruin him and take him down in the world. On the other
hand Judith in having such expectations is having precisely the
same hopes for Allen as his mother does. Furthermore we may

assume that the two families, on the same social level and with children who are friends, are close and work out their responses to the situation together. There is here in other words not just a recipe for a contradiction but a recipe for making it very difficult for the people involved to acknowledge that there is one or recognize it for what it is. And this may be assumed to aggravate the difficulties that could be involved in the transition of the relationship of Allen and Judith from bosom-friends in childhood to sexuality and marriage: to aggravate, that is, the difficulty of seeing and articulating its difficulty.

So a crucial factor is the difficulty of *articulating* (of representing) the difficulty as a difficulty. The poem is most securely tied to its social context by the umbilical cord of language. Having tried to go *through* the poem to a real social situation behind it which it may cryptically represent we are confronted, within that hypothetical real society, by the problem of articulation. What the poem testifies to is not just a crisis of narrative but a crisis, into which this poem about narrative gives us a particular insight, in a narrative idea of life.

This comes out clearly if we examine the treatment of class in the poem. The poem is explicitly about the tight economic circumstances of both families and the problem that presents for marriage. But it does not say *what* class positions or *what* sums of money are involved (in contrast to the contemporaneous treatment of problems of tricky social identification in Austen's novels). For instance:

> 'Oh! could I labour for thee,' *Allen* cried,
> 'Why should our friends be thus dissatisfied?
> On my own arm I could depend, ... '
>
> (88–90)

Here Allen voices a sense of the rather inexplicit social anxieties in the situation. But Crabbe makes him do so in terms which make it impossible to know what social positions are involved.

If we put the emphasis on 'arm' he could be taken to refer to manual labour. But if we read 'arm' metaphorically, and read 'labour' simply as 'work' the objection would be to his relying on what he could earn to support their marriage, even to his working at all. Each reading concerns the anxiety about slipping socially but each reading implies a different set of rungs on the social ladder.

The uncertainty, discussed earlier, about the time-scales involved becomes relevant at this point. For instance does 'The Lovers waited till the time should come,/ When they together could possess a home' (74–5) mean that the time *did* come for which they had been waiting? The eventual outcome would seem to suggest not, but then the next sentence gives another possible reason for that outcome, the objections of Allen's mother to Judith. These objections are introduced in the form of 'Then *Allen*'s mother' which can be taken to mean either 'after that' (after the time had come when they could have, financially, possessed a home) or 'on top of that'. Maybe she was making such objections all the time; maybe she only began to make them when the financial barriers had been overcome; maybe they were silently there all the time entering into the calculations about just what *were* the financial obstacles. The assumption on which the language relies is that just what constitutes a 'home' is as concrete a thing as a house is. 'Till they together could possess a home' is in a sense a model of how the passage and the poem works: a model of the process of displacement, as uncertainties about what they want hide behind uncertainties about whether they will be able to get it. The couple are at a transitional stage of their lives, but the transition will go on for ever. The word that stands out as doing most work in this respect (and which functions in a way that is quite similar to Pip's Expectations in *Great Expectations*) is 'prospect', which occurs three times up to this point:

> As prospects open'd and as life advanc'd,
> They walk'd together, they together danc'd;
>
> (47–8)

> Dull was their prospect — when the Lovers met,
> They said, we must not — dare not venture yet:
>
> (86–7)

> At length a prospect came that seem'd to smile,
> And faintly woo them, from a Western Isle;
>
> (93–4)

The repetition of the word might seem to suggest a stable point of reference at least for changes in how *they think* their lives are going. But in the context of the poem as I have described it the word simply aggravates, by concealing, the difficulties. It can refer to any permutation of the following: the hope of, or certainty of, or possession of an income which might become, or will become, or already is big enough to marry, or to plan to marry, or to hope to marry on. The word can stand as an emblem of a situation which allows and aggravates uncertainty about the strength of desire; of a condition of mirage: a condition and a concept which can allow the man to think he has the guarantee of a wife and a good job when all he really has are uninterrupted visions of a happy future; and to think he faces a miserable future when what he has actually not got is a large income.

The plausibility of discussing people's situations in terms such as 'prospect' does not depend on the assumption that what is specifically referred to in each case (what job, how much money) is even remotely the same. What it does depend on however is the assumption that what is referred to in any particular case would be sufficiently clear, sufficiently known, for its basic ethical meaning to be abstracted into those terms which do posit it as an instance of a general human condition. This does not mean that it assumes a *static* society in which everybody is always what their parents were; indeed the very word 'prospect' implies some degree of mobility, lack of certitude, possibility of change. But it does imply that such lack of certitude, such potentiality, can itself be articulated.

Crabbe's poem is implicated in a set of social relations which seem to encourage the use of this confidently abstracting language, a language designed to help people identify their social place, including their sexual and class place, to characterize themselves. But we can see, in the language of the poem, which leads us through to actual social situations via such crucial words as 'prospect', that it is a social situation which that abstracting language is now itself helping to obfuscate.

The use of the word 'prospect' to refer to possibilities for social advancement is one we can assume that the poem, its characters, and actual early nineteenth-century people were committed to, with all its latent potential for deception and mystification. Another such word is 'fortune' (Allen goes where 'hope and fortune led') which alludes to the notion of 'seeking your fortune'. Ambivalence may indeed be more intrinsic to 'fortune' than to 'prospect': to seek your fortune means both to go and find wealth and to go and find out what fate has in store for you. To use the phrase with any confidence is to commit yourself to self-deception and mystification, a self-deception and mystification which relies, as 'prospect' does, on the reference to the future involved: your refusal to specify which sense of 'fortune' you have in mind depends silently on the very fact that you have not yet found 'it', that you are still seeking.

We have seen then that the poem works through a series of displacements. It displaces the logical problems posed by its first two paragraphs into the substance of the human relationships of the story, and it displaces the uncertainties of the relationships continually into the future. In my analysis I have attempted to track down these displacements, teasing out the ways in which the same problems reappear in slightly altered terms or circumstances. But there is a further dimension to this displacement which needs to be taken into account: a religious one. It first appears in the passage dealing with the parting 'hour' itself:

> But his own *Judith* call'd him to the shore,
> Whom he must meet, for they might meet no more; —
> And there he found her — faithful, mournful, true,
> Weeping and waiting for a last adieu!
> The ebbing tide had left the sand, and there
> Mov'd with slow steps the melancholy Pair:
> Sweet were the painful moments, — but how sweet,
> And without pain, when they again should meet!
> Now either spoke, as hope and fear impress'd
> Each their alternate triumph in the breast.
>
> (121–130)

This passage must surely bring to mind the *simile* of the *rising* tide earlier in the poem. It is as if between that supposedly figurative rising tide of dangerous passion and this supposedly literal ebbing one, there is a hiatus occupied in some way by both sexuality and death; a space of intolerable overlap between two fundamental constituents of mortality, a border-land or no-man's-land, aptly located on the sandy bed of a bay or estuary, both land and sea, neither securely land or sea. The couple's 'last adieu' does indeed seem to be both the last before leaving and the last before death. And of course there would quite openly be such uncertainty: it makes sense for Judith to be, already, 'mournful'. But in that case we must read the more confident 'but how sweet,/ And without pain, when they again should meet' as made possible only by being as applicable to a reunion after death as to an actual reunion in life. It would seem then that the concealed displacement of uncertainties evident particularly in terms such as 'prospect' and 'fortune' has Heaven as its ultimate resource: that place where extremes, life and death, are magically both acknowledged and abolished in

a 'life everlasting' from which mortality — both sexuality and
death — has been removed. It is not that Allen or Judith want
to be or are already dead, but that the idea of heaven makes
possible a concealed ambivalence about the matter.

The role of religious belief becomes more explicit in their
parting conversation. Judith describes her fears for Allen: wars,
diseases,

> 'And women gay, and men are prone to change;
> What then may happen in a year, when things
> Of vast importance every moment brings!
> But hark! An oar!' she cried, yet none appear'd —
> 'Twas love's mistake, who fancied what it fear'd:
> And she continued, — 'Do, my *Allen*, keep
> Thy heart from evil, let thy passions sleep;
> Believe it good, nay glorious, to prevail,
> And stand in safety where so many fail;
> And do not, *Allen*, or for shame, or pride,
> Thy faith abjure, or thy profession hide:
> Can I believe *his* love will lasting prove,
> Who has no rev'rence for the God I love?
> I know thee well! How good thou art and kind;
> But strong the passions that invade thy mind. — ...'
>   (134–48)

The last couplet refers presumably both to the sexual passions al-
luded to earlier, and to emotional protests against religious belief
themselves partly motivated by religious embargoes on sexuality. So once again while sexual and other impulses are to some
extent clearly distinct, they to some extent also overlap. They
overlap in a way which is produced by the degree of unacknowl-
edged separation between them. Allen is 'good and kind' but
also subject to 'invasions' by 'passions'; while she was described
as kind, discreet, and mild, but also 'vain'. It is no wonder that,
contemplating the 'vast gap' of a 'year' she thinks is facing them,

she suggests that 'vast gaps' have characterized the whole course of their relationship, in a form which is paradoxically compatible with a certain reading of the lack of evident change which has been attributed to it: 'things/ Of vast importance every moment brings'.

Judith exploits, in this talk, a very specific imbrication of sexual and religious feelings, one which is by definition not wholly visible. She quite openly wants him to keep both sexual and religious faith of course. But she also uses the first to buttress the second in a way that makes of the second a peculiarly strong external support of the first. And from what Allen says later, in his story-telling to Judith, it does seem as if this bind imposed by Judith has deviously determined his subsequent life. He reports no qualms about his sexual disloyalty to her. But he is evidently divided from his Spanish wife and children by a loyalty to his *religious* faith which is scarcely believable except as a displacement of the *sexual* embargo, since it is totally residual and totally dogged. Giving up his Protestant faith was in fact the condition for fulfilling his sexual and social ambitions. He tried to get round this by 'hiding his profession' without 'abjuring his faith', a compromise which becomes impossible only when his ambitions are realised. But he 'hides his profession' in such a thorough-going fashion (actually professing Catholicism), apparently without qualms, that his eventual inability to 'abjure his faith' comes very strangely. The poem has, it would seem, constructed a situation in which, if Allen is to preserve some continuity with his previous identity (so that in a sense there is no actual 'gap' in his life at all) he has to subvert his new life totally.

The way in which Judith uses God is rather similar to the way in which Allen uses his own mother. And once again the faint outlines of a biblical narrative show through: as Allen goes to God he commits his mother to the protection of his particular love, as Jesus did (and of course he is away for a biblical forty years):

'Upon my Mother,' said the Youth, 'attend;
Forget her spleen, and in my place appear,
Her love to me will make my *Judith* dear;
Oft I shall think, (such comforts lovers seek,)
Who speaks of me, and fancy what they speak;
Then write on all occasions, always dwell
On Hope's fair prospects, and be kind and well,
And ever choose the fondest, tenderest style.'

(150–7)

To ask her to stand in for him in that way, and to write in that fashion whatever she may be feeling or doing is indeed a double-bind, which fits in nicely with the ambivalence of earlier descriptions and, while it does not necessarily determine, could certainly lead to the events of Judith's subsequent life.

The couple at this point reflect each other. I have argued that the poem wants both to confirm and deny a narrative idea of life, and that it does this by a process of continual displacement. The couple's parting dialogue is an example of this process, the couple setting each other up as picture postcards in a covert and self-defeating attempt to ensure the continuity of their lives. They 'frame' each other.

We have already noted how the structure of Allen's most intimate experience on his return forty years later can be described in similarly specular terms. And this is true also of the sequence of events that follows his return. Everything that happens is simply the elaboration of a relationship (first between Allen and the place, and the community, then between Allen and Judith) which is reflexive in the sense that each is the mirror of the other's condition.

Allen 'seems a stranger, and finds all are strange' (284). 'Stranger' there is a powerful word, full of internal conflict. To seem like a stranger but in some ways not to be is to be a strange kind of stranger: he after all finds the people strange not because he does not know them but because he thinks he should or may. Things are that strange only *because* they are that familiar. Of course these are elements always present in the word since there is seldom a situation of total non-recognition. But here we have a situation in which the elements of the word's meaning are also explicit themes of its context, in such a way that the context forces the word to activate its essentially reflexive structure.

The strangeness of what he sees comes over partly in terms of the changed relation between proper names and the people they designate, a change induced by the passage of time. This is another aspect of the historical crisis of 'characterization' to which the poem bears witness. Once people are given their Christian names or are born into their surnames, the names seem to be so much a part of the people that the actually arbitrary relation they bear to the people they name becomes invisible. The mention, at this point in the poem, of the name of Judith's family — "*Flemmings* there were — and *Judith*, doth she live?" asks Allen — which we have not heard before, is startling and full of pathos. This is because our normal experience of the surnames of familiars is subverted. By virtue of the person being lost, totally changed, or dead, their name seems to take over some of their life into its dead form to become the opaque and cryptic sign of an absence. Something similar to this happens in fact to the whole scenario of Allen's native place insofar as it was (insofar as he and we had taken it to be) the natural and inevitable setting for particular known persons. Sea, land, jobs, houses, surnames, and even Christian names now quietly and ruthlessly reveal the very disparate time-scales on which they work, reveal in retrospect, particularly perhaps in a community where the time-scales of all these except individual names could be felt as equally long (equally extended from generation to generation), how easy it was for the individuals Allen and Judith to believe they had all the time in the world.

The names of the dead, separated from those whom they

named and newly visible, are displaced at death into a material
form adjacent to the dead bodies of their erstwhile possessors;
perhaps to prevent the names wandering around as lost souls.
This is the particular conjunction which meets the actually lost
Allen on his return:

> 'The Man is *Allen Booth*, and it appears
> He dwelt among us in his early years;
> We see the name engrav'd upon the stones,
> Where this poor wanderer means to lay his bones.'
>
> (279–82)

Once again Allen sees himself as another. And this reflexive
structure is simply inverted to produce the final relationship of
Allen and Judith:

> Each had immediate confidence; a friend
> Both now beheld, on whom they might depend:
> 'Now is there one to whom I can express
> My nature's weakness, and my soul's distress.'
>
> (297–300)

— a fact emphasized by attributing that final speech to both
of them. And what has to be excised to produce, at last, that
mutual reflection, is clear in the double antithesis which defines
the emphatic 'friend': a friend as distinct from a stranger or
enemy, but also as distinct from a lover. And the relief associated
with the one may belong to the other too.

At an earlier stage in my analysis of this poem I hypothe-
sized a condition of impasse for the couple in which the person
each most naturally desires and wants to marry is also the person
they cannot marry. It is as if in the social world of the Flemmings and Booths there has come to be a fatal degree of overlap
between the kind of person you are allowed to desire — roughly
the same class, in the same area, so long as they are not too
closely related by blood — and the people they are not allowed

to desire or marry — people closely related by blood or of an inferior class. It is as if they are almost part of the same family. And if that seems to be a far-fetched reading we should ponder Crabbe's initial description of the aged couple:

> No wife, nor sister she, nor is the name
> Nor kindred of this friendly Pair the same;
> Yet so allied are they, that few can feel
> Her constant, warm, unwearied, anxious zeal:
>
> (18–21)

This is a riddle. In one sense the poem solves the riddle by telling us their proper names and that they were childhood sweethearts who were separated, married other people, and so on. But there is more to this riddle. It is a description which could well be applied to Adam and Eve, before they acquire the knowledge of good and evil, which is the knowledge of sexual difference. More generally the answer to the riddle would have to be 'anomalous mythical creatures', as Adam and Eve are anomalous mythical creatures: neither kin nor not-kin. It is significant I think that the word 'kindred' is used on two other occasions in the poem:

> Each heart was anxious, till it could impart
> Its daily feelings to its kindred heart;
>
> (50–1)

> Yes! old and griev'd, and trembling with decay,
> Was *Allen*, landing in his native bay,
> Willing his breathless form should blend with
> kindred clay.
>
> (188–90)

In just what sense does Allen feel that all his compatriots are his kin? The poem is preoccupied with this problem. After all, it says that Allen and Judith are not kindred but that they have kindred hearts.

Chapter 11

Kindred

Allen Booth and Peter Grimes seem to identify the societies into which they were born with the families into which they were born. This is not of course how they would put it. It is not how Crabbe would put it either. It is how we may interpret poems which do not fully explain themselves. None of the poems I have discussed so far explain themselves. They are subject to forms of ambivalence and contradiction, like their unhappy protagonists.

In this and in other respects 'The Frank Courtship' is, among Crabbe's poems, the exception that proves the rule. It is Crabbe's great comedy and it brings ambivalence and contradiction out into the open as the subject of its direct and confident attention. It is a confident poem with a confident heroine, whose wishes do not prove vain: the relationship between Sybil Kindred and Josiah will, we feel, go from strength to strength. The more-or-less explicit subject of the poem is that link between the patriarchal and the formal ordering of human life which I have identified as a covert and obscured concern of Crabbe's other poems.

Furthermore, Crabbe's uncertainty as to the reality, the plausibility, of these kinds of order — the patriarchal and the formal — is brilliantly negotiated by 'The Frank Courtship'. The curious Cromwellian remnant which the poem describes is a milieu in which patriarchal order is unusually rigid and explicit but also fragile and theatrical. It is a milieu through which the relation between reality and its formal representation can be explored directly, as a human problem. Elsewhere in his work, I have argued, Crabbe attempts to have his cake and eat it: to assert that life has the structure of a formal representation (a picture, a sequence of portraits, a narrative) and to doubt that it does so. 'The Frank Courtship' successfully transforms the terms of this dilemma so as to suggest that life is — to borrow Alasdair MacIntyre's terms — 'an enacted dramatic narrative in which the characters are also the authors'.[1]

But if 'The Frank Courtship' is a self-possessed poem, in firmer control of its own implications than Crabbe's other poems, this does not mean that it lays down the law as to its own meaning. On the contrary, it actively provokes readers into an awareness of their own participation in the problems to which it refers; into an awareness that its meaning depends upon its historical context and that this context is one which the reader is partly responsible for reconstructing. In my introductory discussion of 'Crabbe's poetry in History' I pointed to the significance of his ambiguous use of certain words — such as 'servant' — which played an important part in the everyday processes of human identification. Here, in 'The Frank Courtship', Crabbe draws active attention to precisely such latent ambiguity in his own and in the everyday use of such identifying terms.

The remarkable self-possession of this poem is indicated right from the start in the surname of its leading family, Kindred:

---

[1] *After Virtue*, p.203.

> Grave *Jonas Kindred*, *Sybil Kindred*'s sire,
> Was six feet high, and look'd six inches higher;
>
> (1–2)

Sybil Kindred has problems, but it is clear from this first couplet — clear to Crabbe and already pretty clear to Sybil — just
what those problems are. Jonas is not only his daughter's father, he is also her king: Crabbe draws attention to these two
meanings of 'sire'. The difference between a father and a king
are important; for instance, you may be able to marry the second but you cannot marry the first. But they may nevertheless
be hard to distinguish, particularly if the two roles seem to be
played by the same person. *The Shorter Oxford English Dictionary* defines 'kindred' as 'the being kin; relationship by blood
(occas., but erron., by marriage)'. This distinction between a
kin relation and a marriage partner is underlined by one of the
dictionary's examples, Pope's line 'Her kindred's wishes and her
sire's commands'. This is a poem in which Sybil, if she is to obey
her father's commands, *almost* has to become his wife. Her father's choice for her is the young Josiah whose name suggests he
is almost 'Jonas her sire'. And in any case she must marry if not
a Kindred, or her kindred, then from among 'the kindred sect':
Crabbe implying, by this usage, that the sect is not much more
than a kinship group:

> They were, to wit, a remnant of that crew,
> Who, as their foes maintain, their Sovereign slew;
> An independent race, precise, correct,
> Who ever married in the kindred sect;
> No son or daughter of their order wed,
> A friend to *England*'s King who lost his head;
> *Cromwell* was still their Saint, and when they met,
> They mourn'd that Saints were not our Rulers yet.
>
> (33–40)

In the last of his *Lectures on the English Poets* (1818-19), 'On
the Lake Poets', Hazlitt offered to explain the poetry of the
Lake School historically, through an analogy between literary
and political revolution:

> Capital letters were no more allowed in print, than
> letters-patent of nobility were allowed in real life;
> kings and queens were dethroned from their rank
> and station in legitimate tragedy or epic poetry, as
> they were decapitated elsewhere:[2]

It looks as if, six years earlier, in those lines from 'The Frank
Courtship', Crabbe has already made the analogy between de-
capitalization and decapitation.

In Crabbe's work, as we have repeatedly noticed, the relationship between proper names and common nouns is problem-
atic. His characters (Richard Monday, Catherine Lloyd, Peter
Grimes, Allen Booth, Judith Flemming) tend to stand in an
insecure relation to their 'proper' names, while the poet's own
descriptions claim the kind of authority — the compulsory relation to what they represent — normally associated with proper
names. 'The Frank Courtship' seems to draw attention to this
link between authority and naming very deliberately. It is not
only Kindred which is decapitalized; Charles I is deprived of
his proper name in the same line which describes his decapitation. Furthermore, by calling the sect 'an independent race'
Crabbe may imply that they are Independents (Congregational-
ists). Implicitly juxtaposing the proper name and the common
noun, he asks us to consider the various senses which the word
'independent' could have for contemporary readers (these senses
were numerous and complicatedly connected: free of the need to
labour, free of aristocratic patronage, free of the state church,
able to support oneself by ones own labour, and so on). Crabbe

---

[2] *The Complete Works of William Hazlitt*, v, pp.143-68 (p.161).

prompts us to an awareness not just of this range of meanings but to an exploration of historical alterations in their relevance to Independents since the name was originally claimed by them in the seventeenth century. Finally, the passage taken as a whole says something about language and meaning in relation to historical changes. Signifiers may have a variety of signifieds, depending on the context in which they are used; but the very fact that there is a continuity of the signifier through alterations of context makes it possible for people (Independents, for instance) to conceal from themselves the fact that signifieds and contexts *have* changed. Crabbe is analysing, in these lines, what is elsewhere an essential feature of his *own* practice. He himself — using the word 'servant' in 'The Parish Register' or 'prospect' in 'The Parting Hour' — trades on a shiftiness in the everyday use of such key words, whose variations of meaning and context are concealed beneath apparent continuity.

It is not only the signifiers of language which provide the formal continuity. Crabbe describes how 'the kindred sect' meet secretly at the Kindred's house, where they turn a craftily constructed china-cabinet to reveal a picture of

> The bold Protector of the conquer'd land;
> Drawn in that look with which he wept and swore,
> Turn'd out the Members and made fast the door,
>   (58–60)

The bold Protector has been separated from his proper name as firmly as the actually decapitated Charles I. What, the poem asks, is the real — that is, the contemporary — meaning of this graven image for the latter-day Saints?

Crabbe shows that the kindred sect — Jonas in particular — represent themselves in terms borrowed from a seventeenth-century and biblical past. Their gestures, language, clothes, pictures, and customary practices, as well as their actual words, are all quotations from this past. But they are quotations out of

context. Whatever their original meanings may have been, they
do not now mean what the sectarians believe they once meant
and still mean. Jonas models himself on Cromwell, but he isn't
a Cromwell. Neither is he the original patriarch Abraham even
though he invokes the Old Testament — '*Sarah* called *Abraham*
Lord' (11) — to justify his tyranny over his own wife.

The ways in which the sect represent themselves are therefore not a wholly true guide to their real character and situation.
It is this discrepancy which Sybil learns to see and make the most
of. She learns how to play a part, to 'dissemble', from her worldly
aunt; but also from observing that her father too plays a part.
She learns 'how fathers are beguil'd' (120). In other words she
learns, as a result of living away from home for some time in her
aunt's household, that her Father (one and only lord and master
of the universe) is in fact only one of a kind, a father who, like
other fathers plays the part of Father. Jonas threatens to turn
Sybil out from under his 'sober roof' (260) if she will not try
to get on with Josiah. But Sybil can see that there is all the
difference in the world between her father purging his house and
Cromwell purging the House of Commons: '"My Aunt", said
Sybil, "will with pride protect/ One whom a Father can for this
reject"' (261–2).

The kindred sect believe they are the heirs of the seventeenth-century 'Saints' and the chosen people of the Old Testament; they believe they are correspondingly set apart from the
worldly society in which they live. They are in fact very distant
from the former and very well integrated with the latter. Indeed they may even have changed sides in the battle they still
think they are waging. 'Cromwell was still their Saint', and don't
they worship his picture as a graven image? They recognize that
things have changed but not how much or in what way they have
changed. 'They mourn'd that Saints were not our Rulers yet':
mourning satisfies them. Theirs is a secular quietism disguised
as a secular pessimism.

These examples seem to suggest a discrepancy between the reality of their situation and the ways in which they represent it to themselves and to others. But, while discrepancies of this kind certainly exist, the relationship between reality and representation revealed by the poem is also more complex.

For instance Crabbe's analysis of the Kindred family and the kindred sect seems to echo Edmund Leach's view, put forward in 'The Legitimacy of Solomon', that the Old Testament is a Levi-Straussian myth designed to mediate a major contradiction. The contradiction is that the Israelites are faced with having to marry outside the tribe (but the race is supposed to be pure) or marrying endogamously (but this entails incest).[3] Even if Joseph is not so much of a Patriarch — an Abraham — as he likes to think, there are similarities.

Furthermore the kindred sect's misrepresentation of themselves is shown to be a necessary and integral part of the reality of their lives. They would not be able to do what they do if they did not sincerely believe they were doing something else. Indeed the tradition they claim to inherit is itself an ambiguous one which makes it more flexible in the present than they would like to admit. One reason why Sybil can reconcile what she wants to do with what her father wants her to do is that there is an egalitarian and proto-feminist element in Independency: Sybil can claim her own independence. There is no simple historical contrast between a patriarchal order which was real in the seventeenth century (even more real in Abraham's time) and a paper-tiger in the present. The judicial execution of Charles I seriously undermined the links which were supposed to bind together fathers of families, the King as Father of his people and God the Father; but it was carried out in the name of a Commonwealth theory which was also, in its own way, patriarchal.

---

[3] *Genesis as Myth and other essays*, pp.25–83 (pp.31, 54–5).

The complexity of the relationship between the reality of
the sect's life and the way in which they represent it is brilliantly evoked by Crabbe's description of Jonas's links with his
worldly sister, Sybil's aunt. It is the existence of this aunt which,
more than anything else, provides Sybil with an alternative to
her father's household and values. But this is only in a special
sense a source of power, a resource, from *outside* the family and
the sect. This worldly kinswoman, on the borders of the immediate family, officially in the sect but not living with them or
living their life, is a crucial figure. It is by going to live with
her that Sybil can get right away from her family without really
doing so. Jonas's thought-processes are fascinating as he won-
ders whether to accede to the aunt's request that Sybil should go
to live with her. He knows something of his sister's reputation
but

> If much of this the graver Brother heard,
> He sometimes censur'd, but he little fear'd;
> He knew her rich and frugal; for the rest,
> He felt no care, or if he felt, suppress'd:
> Nor for companion when she ask'd her Niece,
> Had he suspicions that disturb'd his peace;
> Frugal and rich, these virtues as a charm
> Preserv'd the thoughtful man from all alarm;
> An infant yet, she soon would home return,
> Nor stay the manners of the world to learn;
> Meantime his Boys would all his care engross,
> And be his comforts if he felt the loss.
>
> (87–98)

No explanation of why the aunt asks for Sybil or of why Jonas
thinks it a normal request is given. In effect, Crabbe takes it
for granted as a normal practice, a customary request. That it
may function as a rite of passage is hinted at in the description
of Sybil before she leaves home:

But *Sybil* then was in that playful time,
When contradiction is not held a crime;
When parents yield their children idle praise,
For faults corrected in their after days.

(19–22)

Sybil is sent to her aunt before such correction begins: so perhaps
Jonas is transferring to his sister responsibility for a difficult alteration of relationships. But he'll also transfer it to somebody
whom he half knows may not perform it in the way he would
feel he had to himself. Perhaps the curious fact that he has
christened his daughter Sybil already suggests an ambiguity in
what he wants for her. However that may be, the description
of Jonas's thought-processes as he persuades himself that it is
safe to accede to his sister's request is a brilliant evocation of
self-deception. Each of the grounds for entrusting his daughter
to his sister is, as it comes into his mind, absolutely solid and
adequate. The doubts on a particular point are firmly separated
from the certainty about the very same point ('He felt no care,
or if he felt, suppress'd') and these doubts are taken care of and
suppressed by invoking a new basis for complacency. His mind
moves from one argument to another because he is really not
satisfied with any of them and in order to conceal from himself
that he is not satisfied with any of them. The fact that he has
no certain grounds for confidence can therefore appear to him as
the belief that he has innumerable grounds for confidence. This
continual displacement of anxiety is finally effective because it
moves in circles, a fact which underlines his uncertainty but can
seem to him to underline his certainty. His mind moves out from
'frugal and rich' and comes back to 'frugal and rich' again. This
is a highly controlled use, on Crabbe's part, of that structure we
have observed driving his poetry elsewhere, that 'spiral thinking
which is always trying to hide its own contradiction from itself'.
But the particular contradiction involved here does not only ex-

ist in Jonas's thought. The contradiction, and the mechanisms for mediating and evading it, are powerful in his thought because they are alive in the social context of which he is here the focus.

His sister is of course a kinswoman, which means she is almost by definition a part of the 'kindred sect' to which indeed she nominally belongs. And she is 'frugal and rich' which is a 'virtue' for Jonas because so far as he is concerned it is a trustworthy sign of virtue. Jonas is uncertain because he senses that these equations are not *quite* absolute. But for him to admit openly to himself or others that a frugal and wealthy sister is not necessarily a pious sister in Christ would involve questioning certain fundamental features of his own life. As I say, it is only if the combination of frugality and wealth can be regarded as a reliable sign of virtue that they can, by a simple displacement, be regarded as a virtue in themselves. Crabbe is sharply conscious of the processes by which such semiological duplicity works, and he shows them at work in the Kindred household itself. For instance, in their drawing room 'the plain brown paper lent its decent gloom' (50). What this wallpaper says, and how it says it, are complex. On the face of it the wallpaper says nothing, not only because wallpaper can't speak but because this is very restrained wallpaper. But of course it *can* speak, in the same figurative but true sense in which it can 'lend'. It is restrained, but asserts its restraint, its absolute difference from other, louder, wallpapers. Furthermore, it asserts its *decency*: that it is not licentious or profligate, but that it is not cheap or dowdy either. In fact it asserts the wealth and social position of its owners by the way in which it seems to ignore them.

The distinction between reality and representation can be linked with the distinction, in language itself, between the literal and the figurative. Crabbe's attitude to these distinctions in 'The Frank Courtship' is manifest in the deliberately uncertain figurativeness of his own figures of speech. When Sybil comes home to her parents from her aunt's house she is described in the following terms:

> For she was gay at heart, but wore disguise,
> And stood a Vestal in her Father's eyes;
> Pure, pensive, simple, sad: the Damsel's heart,
> When *Jonas* prais'd, reprov'd her for the part;
> For *Sybil*, fond of pleasure, gay and light,
> Had still a secret bias to the right;
> Vain as she was — and flattery made her vain —
> Her simulation gave her bosom pain.
>
> (129–36)

Sybil's heart and soul draw her back towards the uprightness of the kindred sect (particularly, in the event, to the becomingly upright Josiah) even though they lead her to see the vanities and hypocrisies mingled with it. Crabbe seems to commit himself firmly to a set of fundamental distinctions (between appearance and reality, inside and outside, truth and dissembling, honesty and simulation) which, while they set Sybil somewhat apart from both aunt and father must clearly incline her towards the latter if no other choices are available. The clinching line in this respect is 'Had still a secret bias to the right'. But this phrase which clinches Crabbe's commitment to a familiar range of metaphysical distinctions also subtly questions them. By reviving the dead metaphor from the game of bowls ('bias to the right') Crabbe makes his moral point. But precisely because the source of the metaphor is drawn to our attention there is a suggestion that the opposite of 'right' may only be 'left'. Sybil's bias to it is also an expertise in a game which she is now very good at playing. Her bias to the right is not untainted by the dissembling to which it is so firmly opposed. Of course we cannot be sure how far Crabbe intends this implication to be present. But this uncertainty is itself significant. We cannot be certain how figurative Crabbe's language is here. Figurative language involves the transfer of terms normally used in one context into another context. It is quotation. The kindred sect quote out of context; but is not all quotation the moving of a piece of discourse out of one context and into another? The subtlety of Crabbe's analysis of the relationship between reality and representation in the life of the kindred sect is demonstrated by the fact that his own representation of that relationship is not exempt from the ambiguities to which it refers. Specifically we cannot be certain in this case how far the features of the context (bowls) from which the phrase is taken are to be transferred unaltered into the context in which it is quoted.

The poem's concern with linguistic and behavioural quotation must give a special significance to the passages from Shakespeare's play which introduce it. And two other features of the poem underline this special significance. Firstly, the language which links reality and representation in 'The Frank Courtship' is the language of the theatre (Sybil acts a 'part'). Secondly, the period from which the kindred sect quote — the period of the Civil War and Commonwealth — of course immediately follows the period from which the epigrams are quoted.

The Shakespearian epigrams are as follows:

> Yes, faith, it is my Cousin's duty to make a curtsy, and say, 'Father, as it please you:' but for all that, Cousin, let him be a handsome fellow, or else make another curtsy and say, 'Father, as it pleases me.'
> (*Much Ado About Nothing*, Act II, Scene 1)

> He cannot flatter, he!
> An honest mind and plain — he must speak truth.
> (*King Lear*, Act II, Scene 2)

> God hath given you one face, and you make yourselves another; You jig, you amble, you nick-name God's creatures, and make your wantonness your ignorance.
>
> (*Hamlet*, Act III, Scene 1)

What fire is in mine ears? Can this be true?
Am I contemn'd for pride and scorn so much?
(*Much Ado About Nothing*, Act II, Scene 1)

Like most of Crabbe's Shakespearian epigrams these all offer vivid cameos of individuals or relationships similar to ones we find in the tales they introduce. And they do so on their own, without requiring any knowledge of the original Shakespearian contexts. Thus the first passage is analogous to Sybil's position (and perhaps to her Aunt's advice to her), her determination to do what her father wants her to do unless she can't make that coincide with what she herself wants to do. The second passage would refer to Josiah and perhaps to Sybil's taunting of Josiah; while the third refers to Josiah's castigation of Sybil. The fourth also refers to the splendid encounter between the two, either to Sybil as she listens to Josiah or Josiah as he listens to Sybil.

These analogies are clearly there. But something very odd happens to them if we put the quotations back into their original contexts; contexts which Crabbe indicates (by citing play, act, and scene) but does not describe. He does not tell us who says them, when, or to whom. If we remember or seek out these contexts we discover that all of the speeches except the first are spoken to or about people who are dissembling, putting on an act. The passage from *King Lear* is spoken by Regan's husband the Duke of Cornwall, and spoken, sarcastically, of the Earl of Kent who has arrived in the guise of a common follower and messenger of Lear. The passage from *Hamlet* is spoken by Hamlet to Ophelia, who has been set up by Claudius and Polonius who are watching the course of the encounter from hiding. And the issue of dissimulation and role-playing is even more complicated in this scene of course if Hamlet is aware of the stratagem and is therefore himself 'acting' for the benefit of the same hidden audience. Finally, the lines from *Much Ado About Nothing* are spoken by Benedict who thinks he is eavesdropping on what is in fact a set-up disclosure of invented professions of love for him by Beatrice. The significance of the event in this last case is that Beatrice and Benedict have got into the position of being, for each other, the very public symbols of the refusal of each to marry anybody. Their friends believe (correctly as it turns out) that simulated, imaginary events have to be laid on by others if the couple are to be released from that bind into a recognition of the affection which is clearly generated by their sparring. So this final passage, in its Shakespearian context, is an example of the creative value of 'acting', of fictional behaviour in everyday life as a means for enabling people to do things and discover feelings which they would not otherwise be able to do or discover (what did Austen's Fanny Price think of 'The Frank Courtship'?). The passage from *Hamlet* too of course is an instance of how one may 'by indirections find directions out'; but in this case it is a moot point whether the multiplication of such stratagems releases the truth or compounds the sense of confusion and unreality. And Kent's strategy has a similarly ambiguous result.

So these passages from Shakespeare have one kind of relationship to Crabbe's poem if we know their original context and another if we do not know that context. Both readings make sense, but you cannot make both readings at once. In other words Crabbe's use of these quotations enacts (to use an overused literary-critical term which here seems unusually appropriate) the risky but potentially productive duplicity to which, in their original contexts, they refer. Just as 'chosen friends' can turn the china-cabinet to reveal Cromwell so inquisitive readers can make the Shakespearian epigrams look very different by seeking out the passages of text from which they have been removed.

Crabbe's investigation of the part which acting — linguistic and behavioural quotation — plays in the construction of real life reaches its climax at the end of the poem in the long encounter between Sybil and Josiah. Jonas leaves them together with stern hints to Sybil that she must like Josiah:

> Silent they sate — thought *Sybil*, that he seeks
> Something, no doubt; I wonder if he speaks;
> Scarcely she wonder'd, when these accents fell
> Slow in her ear — 'Fair Maiden, art thou well?' —
> 'Art thou Physician?' she replied; 'my hand,
> My pulse at least shall be at thy command.'
>
> She said, and saw, surpris'd, *Josiah* kneel,
> And gave his lips the offer'd pulse to feel;
> The rosy colour rising in her cheek,
> Seem'd that surprise unmix'd with wrath to speak;
> Then sternness she assum'd, and — 'Doctor, tell,
> Thy words cannot alarm me, — am I well?'
>
> 'Thou art,' said he, 'and yet thy dress so light,
> I do conceive, some danger must excite:'
>
> (364–77)

Sybil is not in control of the consequences of her aggressively defensive irony; partly because Josiah shows himself capable of understanding irony and responding in kind, partly because of the precariousness of any irony, and partly because of the specific subject matter of the irony in this case. The irony in the passage, and in the ensuing dialogue, is precipitated by the question 'Art thou Physician?' and hinges on the double-meaning, or diverse associations, of the words 'hand', 'pulse', 'well' and so on. Sybil and Josiah are playing doctors; by means of this sustained irony, this play-acting, Sybil and Josiah speak and learn a great deal of truth to and from each other. It is ironic but true to describe this as a frank courtship. If this sustained irony (irony of gesture and action as much as speech) is a kind of play-acting it is important to define just what sort of play-acting it is and just why they find themselves acting in this particular play. It is not the kind of acting in which (as in the passages from Shake-

speare) people are wholly intent on deception of themselves or
each other; nor are Sybil and Josiah suspending, or requiring
each other to suspend, disbelief as in the relationship between
the players and the audience at Shakespeare's plays. But elements of both these kinds of acting are involved, for Sybil and
Josiah are not 'only pretending', if by this we mean that each
remains wholly unchanged and intact behind the roles they deliberately and obviously adopt. Though both imply that this *is*
the case: both have pretensions to be only pretending and there
is a degree of complicity between them in this respect.

'Art thou Physician?' is ironic in the sense that it is a
sarcastically rhetorical question. Sybil is then drawn to pursue
this fictional relationship, and Josiah to respond in kind, and we
need to work out why this particular fictional relationship, the
doctor-patient relationship, should be so helpful to them. One
reason is surely that it is a relationship between the body of one
person and the gazing, examining eye of another, but a relationship which is nevertheless impersonal, professional, proper. In
other words it is a relationship which is very close to a sexual
one but in which the sexual is designed to be as firmly absent
as possible. From one point of view then they start to play doctors as a means of sublimation, to banish sexuality by throwing
cold water on it. At the same time, since they are not in fact
doctor and patient, to pretend that they are risks provoking sexual feeling, enabling it to emerge very powerfully just because
they are 'only pretending'. Precisely because playing doctors is
a risky business they are as much the servants as the masters
of its logic, as is splendidly demonstrated in the passage I have
quoted. Sybil offers Josiah a purely medical 'hand' for exam-
ination. The words and gesture of the patient to the (socially
inferior) doctor are borrowed to contain a relationship which
could become sexual. But in their situation the literal medical
'hand' must recall the metaphorical 'hand' that is given in marriage. The conjunction of the two meanings makes suddenly and

surprisingly visible the literal erotic hands of the lover. Sybil, sensing that, shifts quickly to 'my pulse, at least', a shift which, as Josiah's subsequent gesture and her own embarrassed blushes show, aggravates the feelings it is designed to disinfect.

If she is to remain a part of the kindred sect, to obey her father, Sybil must get engaged to Josiah. If she is to do what she wants to do she must almost certainly not get engaged to him. She would if it were possible like to do both. Her initiation of the play is designed, in so far as it is designed, to subvert her father's intentions. But it is also, as it turns out, very well designed to enable her to fulfil the wishes of both her father and herself. The punning conjunction of the roles they have been organized to play (intended marriage partners) and the fictional roles they adopt (doctor and patient) generates desire.

There is one further aspect of the exchange between the couple which needs explaining. I have suggested that for the poet who juxtaposes Kindred and kindred, though perhaps not for the characters in his poem, an important element in the impasse facing Sybil is the conflict between kin endogamy (required for religious, social, and quasi-ethnic reasons) and the incest taboo. Sybil and Josiah's playing at doctors seems to me to support this contention. John Berger points out that it is just because of the similarity between the relationship of doctor to patient and the relationship between lovers that all medical ethics make a positive promise of 'physical intimacy without a sexual basis'. But, he asks,

> what can such intimacy mean? Surely it belongs to the experiences of childhood. We submit to the doctor by quoting to ourselves a state of childhood and simultaneously extending our sense of family to include him. We imagine him as an honorary member of the family.[4]

---

[4] *A Fortunate Man*, p.62.

If this is the case then Sybil and Josiah are involved in an aspect of the poem of which its characters have not up to this point been aware.

The couple are quoting a relationship which itself (as Berger points out) quotes a familial relationship. The couple quote this relationship because it enables them to sublimate sexuality. But it also, I have suggested, risks manifesting this sexuality. It does so however not only for the reason I have previously suggested — that they are not in reality doctor and patient — but also because, just like doctor and patient, they are *not* in fact kin. Their role-playing can therefore bring into the open, simultaneously, a sense that they are kin and, in consequence, a real knowledge of the significance of the fact that they are not.

Most of Crabbe's young women are more like the Fanny of 'Delay has Danger' than they are like Sybil. But like both Fanny and Sybil they go to live with aunts, or 'aunts', older women who are outside their immediate family circle but related to one of the parents by blood or marriage or some early association. These older women are very often wealthier than the girl's own parents, one or both of whom are usually dead. The nature of these relationships between the girls and the other women is not clearly spelt out for them or for us. Nobody can be quite sure whether these are essentially familial, or economic or even sexual relationships. Are the girls adopted daughters, servants, lovers, or what? These older women are on the line which divides kin from not-kin, the girl's own class from another class. Their function is implicitly the traditional one of helping the girl make the transition from the family in which she was born to the family she will form by marriage. But in these stories of rites of passage that fail, the aunts, for reasons that always remain partly obscure, prevent rather than enable the transition. The girls seem to be trying simultaneously to reconstitute and to leave their family of origin. Like their male counterparts, they are stuck on border land.

By contrast, Sybil Kindred successfully passes through her rite of passage. The loss of secure identity, the ambivalence, which is at the centre of such rites is for her a positive experience. I have described in detail some of the reasons why this should be so. Many of the difficulties which cannot be clearly formulated in the other poems are clearly present, as difficulties, here. But there is one difficulty which is not present in 'The Frank Courtship'. Sybil never has to worry about what class she is in. Differences between worldly and unworldly sections of the same class — cultural differences — take the place of those uncertainties about money and status which help to blight the lives of so many inhabitants of Crabbe's border land. On this occasion, when the border is not a social stratification line, it is crossed with confidence.

Index

STUDIES IN BRITISH LITERATURE

Learning Resources
Centre